# HISTORY STORIES FOR PRIMARY GRADES

by

*John W. Wayland*

**YESTERDAY'S CLASSICS**

**ITHACA, NEW YORK**

This edition, first published in 2022 by Yesterday's Classics, an imprint of Yesterday's Classics, LLC, is an unabridged republication of the text originally published by The Macmillan Company in 1919. For the complete listing of the books that are published by Yesterday's Classics, please visit www.yesterdaysclassics.com. Yesterday's Classics is the publishing arm of Gateway to the Classics which presents the complete text of hundreds of classic books for children at www.gatewaytotheclassics.com.

ISBN: 978-1-63334-163-0

Yesterday's Classics, LLC
PO Box 339
Ithaca, NY 14851

# PREFACE

THE pedagogical value of the story has always been recognized but is now being utilized more fully, perhaps, than ever before. At the same time, the need for a suitable variety of story materials and story forms is growing apace. This is especially true in the child's field of history. The need for real history stories, simple enough for little children, is keenly felt every day by teachers in the schools and by parents in the homes.

To meet this need, in some measure, the stories in this little book have been prepared. They are intended primarily for the use of the teacher and the parent in oral instruction, but they may also be read in due time by the child himself. Accordingly, the writer has aimed to adapt them to the uses contemplated, not only in subject matter but also in diction, style, and length.

The subjects have been chosen mainly from the history of our own country, but a few Old World stories have been included. The characters are few and distinct: they are women as well as men, girls as well as boys. Industrial and social conditions are portrayed along with those hitherto more conventional.

Easy phases of geography and literature are incorporated; and, as far as possible, simple yet attractive titles have been applied.

A studious effort has been made to simplify and unify these stories by leaving out those details and circumstances that would only distract the child, and to make them vital and vivid by enlarging such details as serve the main purpose.

The morals are not pointed, as a rule, but they are obvious enough in most cases, it is believed, to be seen.

One of the secrets of interest in teaching children is to be found in seizing the time and the occasion. Therefore, a large number of these little stories have been especially adapted for use in connection with the various holidays and anniversaries that fall within the school year, and may be used in an order following the annual calendar rather than in the order in which they appear in the book.

At the end of some of the stories are supplementary notes addressed to the teacher. These are intended to supply additional information at convenient places and to embody certain specific suggestions, in the hope of practical helpfulness. The author also ventures in this place to refer the teacher to his handbook, *How to Teach American History,* particularly to Chapter XI: "The Use of the History Story in the Teaching of History."

It will be observed that this collection of stories has been made to answer the requirements of the first three years as set forth in the report of the Committee of Eight. Accordingly, the large number of teachers who are following the plan of this committee will find this book of special value.

# CONTENTS

## PART ONE

## PART TWO

# PART THREE

# THE FIRST CHRISTMAS SONG

Some angels sang the first Christmas song, and some shepherds heard it.

It was one night, long, long ago; and it was in a country far, far away.

In that country the people kept a great many sheep. The men and boys who took care of the sheep were called shepherds.

The shepherds would take the sheep out where the grass was green, and keep them there all day. They would keep a sharp watch so that nothing would come out of the woods and hurt the sheep. Often they would lead the sheep down by the brooks, where the cool, clear water went tumbling over the stones, and where they could find nice shady places under the trees.

Sometimes the shepherds would camp out with the sheep. They would stay out in the fields and watch the sheep all night. Cattle and sheep often like the nighttime for grazing better than the daytime.

*In the Fields One Night*

But I started to tell you about the first Christmas song.

Well, in that land so far away, some shepherds were out in the fields one night, keeping watch over their flock.

All at once they thought it was morning, but it wasn't. It grew light—just as light as day—but it wasn't morning. The light came all at once; and when the shepherds saw the great light, and found that it wasn't morning, they didn't know what to think of it. They didn't know what to do. They were frightened, terribly frightened.

And then they saw somebody. Somebody stood right before them in the great light. It was an angel, and he began to speak to them. He said:

"Don't be afraid! I bring you good news. I come to make you happy. It is Christmas!"

And then the shepherds saw more angels. A great crowd of angels stood right before them in the bright light. And then the angels began to sing. These are the words they sang:

"Glory to God in the highest,
    And on earth peace, good will toward men."

It was the first Christmas song! The angels sang it, and I imagine that the shepherds learned to sing it, too. Every Christmas, nowadays, a great many people sing that song.

Is it not a beautiful song? Don't you think it ought to make the world happy?

# THE FIRST EASTER MORNING

It will soon be Easter, so to-day I'm going to tell you a little Easter story.

It was in a city far away, and it was early in the morning. Three or four good women were going along the street. It was before daylight—it was still dark—and it may be that those good women were afraid; but they went on.

It was Sunday morning, and the women were going to the cemetery. You have seen persons going to the cemetery on Sunday, with flowers, have you not? They put the flowers on the grave of some friend.

Well, those good women had a dear friend who had died. His name was Jesus, and he had been laid in the cemetery two or three days before. They were going to visit his grave. They were carrying spices and perhaps flowers, too.

Now, what do you think? They expected to find it dark at the grave, but it was light. They expected to find the vault locked, but it was open. They thought that the body of their friend would still be there, but it was gone!

At the tomb was an angel. He said to the women "You are looking for Jesus, aren't you? He is not here."

Best of all, the angel told the women that Jesus was not dead—that he had risen from the dead.

All this frightened the women very much, but it also made them very happy. They were so glad that their dear friend was alive, and that they should see him again!

And it was not long till they did see him. He came to them and talked with them. He made them all very happy.

Now, that was the first Easter morning. It was the first Sunday morning. It was a morning of joy. Easter Sunday should be a day of joy to all of us.

# THE GIRL WHO HEARD VOICES

Once a girl lived close to a beautiful tree. It was called the Lady's Tree. People thought that good fairies often came to play around that beautiful tree.

The girl's name was Joan. One day when Joan was near the Lady's Tree she heard voices. They seemed to speak to her, and she listened.

It was not many days till Joan heard the voices again. By that time she was pretty certain that the voices were speaking to her. As she listened she heard them tell her to do something—something that was very hard to do. The voices told her to go and drive a big army out of France.

France was Joan's own country. Joan loved France dearly. But thousands of soldiers from another country had been in France for a long time. They had killed and hurt many of Joan's friends. Even Joan's king had scarcely a safe place to live.

But Joan heard the voices say:

"Go! Drive those soldiers out of France! Go! Save your king and put the crown upon his head!"

# The Girl Who Heard Voices

When Joan told her father and mother about the voices they laughed at her and scolded her. They said:

"You are dreaming! You did not hear any voices! If you did, they were bad voices."

But Joan was certain that she did hear voices. And she believed that they were good voices. Whenever she went near the beautiful Lady's Tree she heard the voices speaking to her.

At last Joan said: "I must obey the voices. They are calling me. They are giving me work that I ought to do."

And at last her father and mother let her go. She mounted a horse and rode away to the king.

At first the king laughed at Joan, too. And all the king's men laughed. They said, "How foolish the girl must be!"

But Joan said: "I hear the voices. They speak to me. They say to me that I must drive the enemy out of France and put the crown on the king's head."

Joan was so brave and true that the king and his men began to trust her. They said:

"If you will go in front we will follow you. We will go and drive the enemy out of France."

Then Joan mounted a strong white horse. She took a big white banner in her hand and rode in front of the king's army. She waved the banner and the men fought bravely.

It was a long, hard fight, but the king's men won.

Joan waved the white banner and led them till they won a great victory.

Then Joan took the young king and led the way to a great church. There in that great church the crown was placed on the young king's head. A wonderful day it was. Everybody said:

"The king is crowned! France is saved! It was a good voice from heaven that Joan heard!"

When Joan saw that the king was crowned she said:

"Now let me go home. Let me go home to my mother and father—to my white sheep and lambs—to the beautiful Lady's Tree!"

But everybody said, "No! No! You must mount the white horse and carry the white banner again. You must lead our men till all the foes of France are driven out."

The king and his men felt that they could not fight without Joan to carry the white banner and lead them.

But one day when Joan was leading some of the king's men they did not stand by her. They let her fall into the hands of the enemy, who put her to death.

It was a sad day for France when Joan died, but the brave men of France did not forget her. They fought on, day after day, till all the foes were driven out. They remembered the pure white banner and the girl who heard the voices. They said:

"She still leads us!"

# A ROOM FULL OF GOLD

Once, a long time ago, some robbers met the king of Peru. The robbers were led by an old man named Pizarro. Pizarro was very brave, but he was a bad man. He was very cruel and wicked.

The king was a young man, tall and strong; and he, too, was very brave. I think that he was a much better man than Pizarro.

The king had many soldiers, Pizarro had only a few; but Pizarro and his men had guns and horses.

The king of Peru and his people had never seen horses before. They thought that the horses were terrible creatures, and feared them greatly. And when they heard the sound of the guns, and saw the smoke and the fire burst from them, they were frightened more than ever.

Because Pizarro and his men had guns and horses they were able to beat the young king's men and to take the king himself prisoner. Then they shut the poor young king up in a big room.

One day when Pizarro went in to see the king, the king said:

"If you will set me free I'll give you a room full of gold."

Then the tall young king stood up beside the wall and put his hand up as far as he could. When he had his hand up as high as he could reach he made a mark on the wall.

"See," he cried, "I'll give you this big room full of gold up to that mark if you will set me free."

He did not know how mean and cunning old Pizarro was.

The gold was just what Pizarro wanted. He knew that Peru was a rich country and that the king had a great deal of gold; so he said:

"All right. You have the room filled with gold up to that mark and I'll set you free."

Then the young king was glad. He called his men and sent them out to get the gold. Here and there, far and near, they hurried, asking for gold for the king. All the gold they could find was brought and put into the big room.

It took a long time. One day was not enough, for gold is very heavy and some of it had to be carried for miles and miles. Much of it had to be taken across high mountains, for there are many huge mountains in Peru.

One month was not enough. It took the king's men two, three, four, five, six months to get enough gold to fill the big room.

But at last the room was full—clear up to the mark

on the wall that the tall young king had made.

Pizarro and his men laughed and rubbed their hands in glee when they saw so much gold. They had not dreamed that there was so much gold in all Peru.

And now, what do you suppose Pizarro did with the brave young king?

He did not set him free, as he had promised to do, but he kept him in prison and at last put him to death.

For Pizarro was a robber—he was a wicked, cruel man. We could not expect such a man to keep his word. He cared only for the room full of gold.

# BABY VIRGINIA

I am going to tell you about a baby girl named Virginia. She was born long, long ago, on an island.

Do you know what an island is? It is a piece of land with water all around it. There are many islands in the world, some large, some small.

The island on which Baby Virginia lived is nine miles long and three miles wide. It is called Roanoke Island, and it is now a part of the state of North Carolina. It lies on the eastern side of the state, near the ocean.

Baby Virginia's birthday came in the month of August. Her father's name was Ananias—Ananias Dare; so her full name was Virginia Dare. Her mother's name was Eleanor—Eleanor Dare; and her grandfather's name was John—John White.

On Sunday, when Baby Virginia was taken to church the first time, everybody was glad. They were so glad to see a little white baby. She was the first white baby ever born on the island. In fact, she was the first white baby ever born in this country, so far as we know.

There were plenty of brown babies—Indian babies— on the island, but the Indians, too, were glad to see Baby Virginia. That first Sunday, when she was taken to church, some of the Indians were there, too.

After some days Virginia's grandfather got on a ship and sailed away. He said, "I'll not be gone long."

But he was gone a long time. He had to sail clear across the ocean. That took a long time in those days. When he got across the ocean he found a war going on. This war kept him from going back to the island to see Baby Virginia. It was three years before he got back.

When he did get back to the island Baby Virginia was gone. Her father and her mother were gone, too. All the white people were gone.

Nobody knows what became of Baby Virginia. Her grandfather hunted for her a long time, but he could not find her.

Now a great many people live on the island and they often think of little Virginia Dare. And every August, when her birthday comes around, they have a party in her honor and talk about her.

# SQUANTO, THE CORN-PLANTER

Squanto was an Indian. He taught the white people how to plant corn.

When William Bradford and Miles Standish and other white people came to this country they found some corn in a basket. The Indians had grown the corn and had made the basket. But when they saw the white men they were frightened and ran away.

Some of the ears of corn in the basket were yellow, some were red, and some had blue and yellow grains mixed. The white men thought that the ears of corn were very beautiful, but they did not know how to make corn grow.

After a while some of the Indians came back. One of them was Squanto. Squanto could speak some words of English, for he had once been carried on a white man's ship to England. Squanto liked the white men and came to live with them.

And when spring came Squanto taught the white men how to plant corn. He watched the trees in the forest, and when the little green leaves on the oak trees and the hickory trees were about as big as a squirrel's ear he said, "Now is the time to plant corn."

He showed the white men how to dig up the ground and how far apart to make the hills. Then he showed them how to drop in the grains of corn and how deep to cover them with earth.

But before Squanto covered the hills of corn he did a curious thing. What do you suppose he did? He caught a fish and put it into a hill of corn. He caught a great many fishes, so as to have one or two for each hill of corn. Then, after he had dropped a fish or two into each hill, with the grains of corn, he covered them with earth.

Squanto put the fish into the hills of corn to make the corn grow fast and to make the stalks grow tall and strong. The Indians often used fish in this way to make their corn grow.

For two or three weeks after the corn was planted men had to watch the cornfields day and night, to keep the wolves away. What do you think the wolves wanted? They wanted the fish. Nowadays farmers sometimes have to watch their cornfields in the daytime to keep the crows away. The crows want the corn. But in the days of Squanto wolves were numerous and they wanted the fish. If they had not been kept away they would have come and dug up fish, corn, and all.

Do not forget Squanto, the corn-planter.

# THANKSGIVING DAY

Do you know how many days it will be till Thanksgiving?

Let us get the calendar and see.

How many of you remember last Thanksgiving Day?

Every year, for many years, the good people of our land have kept Thanksgiving Day. It comes in the month of November, after the corn, the apples, and the pumpkins are gathered, and after the farmers have cut a pile of wood big enough to last all winter.

By that time, too, the boys and girls who live in the country have had a chance to gather shellbarks and walnuts, and the squirrels, out in the woods, have filled the hollow trees with nuts and acorns.

Then everybody feels that God has been very good. He has sent the rain and the sunshine, and has made the corn and the apples and the nuts grow. So we have Thanksgiving Day.

Sometimes a snow comes about Thanksgiving time. Then we ought to remember the little birds, and put out something for them to eat. We ought also to remember poor people and try to make them happy.

*The Feast at Plymouth Town*

Do you know why they had pumpkin pies at the first Thanksgiving, long ago?

It was because they had no apples. So they took the big yellow pumpkins and made pies of them. Now we have had pumpkin pies at Thanksgiving so many times that we do not want to do without them.

The first Thanksgiving was at a place called Plymouth. For almost a year the people there had been very hungry. When autumn came and they had more to eat they felt very thankful. So they had a big thanksgiving feast.

They had pumpkin pies, as I have told you. They also had turkey, because the woods were then full of fat wild turkeys. And they had venison. Do you know what venison is? Venison is deer meat.

The white men shot deer and turkeys with their guns. The Indians shot deer and turkeys with their bows and arrows. Then the white men and the Indians feasted together.

What a pity that the white men and the red men were not always good friends, as they were at the first Thanksgiving!

That first Thanksgiving feast at Plymouth lasted three days. But soon people were too busy to take so much time. As far back as I can remember—and much farther, I guess—the Thanksgiving feast has lasted only one day each year.

Now you may listen to a little rhyme. It will help you to remember about that first Thanksgiving at Plymouth.

> Night and morn
> Shocks of corn
> Stood 'round Plymouth Town;
> Then a freeze
> Nipped the trees,
> And the nuts came down.
>
> Late that fall
> Indians tall
> Came to Plymouth Town,
> There to eat
> Corn bread sweet
> And turkey roasted brown.
>
> Ready there
> Maidens fair
> Served at Plymouth Town—
> Cakes and pies,
> Bakes and fries,
> And turkey roasted brown!

All the men
Quickly then
To the feast sat down;
Three whole days
Thanks and praise
Rose at Plymouth Town.

# WASHINGTON'S BIRTHDAY

Long ago, in a big house beside a big river, lived a man named George Washington. Have you heard your fathers and mothers speak of him? Have you seen his picture? Here is one.

*George Washington*

To-day, near the place where Washington lived, is a beautiful city named Washington.

All over our land to-day the people love Washington. They love him because he was a good man—a great man—and because he did so much to help our country. Every year now, when the month of February comes around, we celebrate Washington's birthday.

How many of you have a birthday in February? Well, even if your birthday does not come in this month remember that Washington was born in February.

I told you that Washington lived in a big house beside a big river. That was when he was a man. He was born in another house. The house in which he was born stood beside the same big river, but it was not a large house. It had only four rooms and an attic. At each end was a huge chimney. Inside were wide fireplaces. Don't you imagine that the children had lots of fun in the winter evenings, popping corn in those big fireplaces?

George's father had a long name Augustine. His mother had a short name—Mary. You can all remember that.

When George was three years old the family went to live at another place—in another house. But this house was also beside the big river. It was the place where Washington lived when he was a man. Near it now is the beautiful city, as I told you.

I do not know just when George learned to swim, but it was not long till he was a good swimmer. I judge that his father taught him to swim; or perhaps he was taught by one of his older brothers. He could also run fast, and ride a horse, and wrestle, and climb a tree. He could outrun and outswim and outride and outwrestle all the boys he played with, but they all liked him because he was kind and played fairly. And he always told the truth.

I suppose that George soon learned to catch fish in that big river. I am pretty certain that his brothers had a boat, and they all perhaps got into the boat when they went fishing.

When George was seven years old his parents moved again. They went to live in another house. This makes three houses, does it not, by the time George was seven? In the first house he was born, and there he lived till he was three years old. In the second house he lived for the next four years or so; then, when he was seven, he went to the third house. I can see him walk in, find a peg or a nail for his hat, and say: "This is my new home."

This home was also beside a river. But it was not the same big river he had seen at the other places. It was a much smaller river, but it had a longer name. The big river was the Potomac; the smaller one was the Rappahannock. These are both Indian names; and there were plenty of Indians in the country when George Washington was a little boy.

# A BIG BELL

I am going to tell you about a big bell that I once saw. It is an old, old bell, and it has a long crack in it. Somebody struck it too hard. It is a very famous bell. Nearly every schoolboy, nearly every schoolgirl in this country has heard of it. Some day you may see it.

I had often heard of this bell, and one morning I happened to be in the city where it is kept. I went around to a big brick house and waited at the front door. It was almost nine o'clock.

Just as the clock struck nine the door opened and I walked in. Right in front of me was the big old bell. It is as tall as a man and it is as heavy as a ton of coal. It hangs fast to a strong old piece of wood, but it does not ring any more. It is cracked badly enough now. If it were rung again it might crack still more.

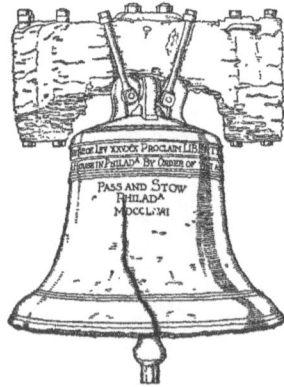

*Liberty Bell*

This old bell is called Liberty Bell. It got that name many years ago when our grandfathers were fighting in a war to win their liberty. In those days it was rung

24

often. On the bell are some words from the Bible. They say something about liberty too. Old Liberty Bell is very dear to all our people.

Sometimes old Liberty Bell is put on the train and carried to other cities. Once it was taken to Chicago. At another time it was taken to San Francisco—thousands and thousands of miles. Wherever the train would stop great crowds of people would come up and try to get a glimpse of this famous bell.

Sometime, when you are older, I shall tell you more about Liberty Bell.

Now, let us learn this little rhyme:

> Liberty Bell, Liberty Bell,
> Once again your story tell;
> One, two, three,
> Ring for me,
> Ring and ring, O Liberty Bell!
>
> Liberty Bell, Liberty Bell,
> I would know your story well;
> One, two, three,
> O'er land and sea,
> Ring and ring, O Liberty Bell!

# NANCY HART'S DINNER

Nancy Hart lived in Georgia, long ago. Her house was a little cabin, away out in the wild woods. She and her children lived in that cabin in the woods, but they were not afraid.

Nancy was tall and strong. She was over six feet in height, and she was stronger than some men. She was also very brave, and she could ride a horse and shoot a gun. She would shoot deer, catch fish, and trap rabbits and other animals. In these ways she got food for herself and her children. I suppose she also had a garden in which she grew corn, potatoes, and maybe some watermelons. You know Georgia is a great place for watermelons.

One day five soldiers came to Nancy Hart's cabin. It was war time, and soldiers were all over the country.

Those five soldiers who came to Nancy Hart's cabin had on red coats. That meant that they were British soldiers. Nancy did not like British soldiers, but she did not tell them so.

She smiled and said, "Come in."

She had a sweet voice.

The soldiers came in.

"We want dinner," they said.

"All right," replied Nancy, "sit down and rest. I'll get dinner for you in a jiffy."

She flew around and soon had dinner on the table. The redcoats were much pleased. "She is our friend," they thought. They stood their guns up against the wall and sat down to dinner.

Nancy waited on them in fine style. She was here, there, and everywhere, just as polite as she could be. The soldiers thought:

"What a good dinner! What a nice time we are having!"

But the next thing they knew Nancy had hidden their guns! Then she stood in the door and said, "Finish your dinner, gentlemen, you are my prisoners."

When two of them tried to get away she shot them. Then the other three sat still.

One thing that helped Nancy was the fact that she was cross-eyed. This is what people say; and so they say that the British soldiers couldn't tell which way she was looking; they couldn't tell which way she might shoot next time.

Nancy sent word to her neighbors and they came to help her. Not one of the five soldiers got away.

The people of Georgia love Nancy Hart because she was brave and because she did what she could to help her country.

# BETSY ROSS'S NEEDLE

I am going to tell you about Betsy Ross and what she did with her needle.

Betsy Ross was a pretty young woman. Her husband was dead. He had been a soldier and had died in the army.

Mrs. Ross lived in a little house in a big town. The town was Philadelphia. Can you say "Philadelphia"?

Betsy Ross could sew well. She made nice things with her scissors and her needle.

One day three gentlemen called at Betsy Ross's house. One of those gentlemen was General George Washington. Those gentlemen wanted Mrs. Ross to make a flag—a nice, new flag, with stars and stripes on it.

General Washington told Mrs. Ross what he thought would make a nice flag. He showed her what kind of stars he would make.

The stars he made had six points. Mrs. Ross said:

"General, stars do not have six points—they have only five points."

With her sharp scissors Mrs. Ross clipped out a star with five points.

When General Washington saw it he said:

"You are right, madam; make the stars with five points."

After the gentlemen left Mrs. Ross worked fast on the new flag. She put on it long stripes of white and red. In one corner she sewed on a big square of blue, and on the square of blue she sewed thirteen white stars. Each of the white stars had five points.

*Mrs. Ross and the Flag*

When General Washington and the other gentlemen saw the new flag they were very much pleased with it. They said that it was a fine flag and that Mrs. Ross was a good hand at making flags.

Betsy Ross had no sewing machine (nobody had sewing machines in those days), but she made her fingers fly. Her needle seemed to dance merrily on the red and the white and the blue.

Mrs. Ross made many other flags, just like the first one. Our flags to-day are very much like those she made.

The red in the flag means that our people should be brave; the white means that they should be good; and the blue means that they should be true.

> With needle and with thread,
> She sewed the stripes of red;
> She made them fit just right
> Beside the stripes of white.
>
> She made a square of blue,
> Because good men are true;
> She made the stars of white,
> Because they give us light.

# A WHITE HORSE

You have all seen white horses, I suppose, but I am going to tell you about a white horse that was very famous. He became famous because he belonged to a famous man. Some day you will read about him in the history books for yourselves.

This white horse had a long name. He was called Traveler. I suppose he was given this name because he could get over the ground in a hurry.

This famous white horse, Traveler, belonged to General Robert Lee. General Lee rode him during the war between the Blue and the Gray, and all the soldiers in gray knew Traveler almost as well as they knew General Lee.

They called General Lee "Marse Robert"; and whenever "Marse Robert" would get on Traveler and ride along the road all the soldiers would wave their hats and cheer. Traveler became so used to this sort of thing that he did not mind it much. I suspect that "Marse Robert" minded it more than Traveler did.

At last the war was over, and General Lee went to Lexington to teach school. This Lexington is in

Rockbridge County, Virginia; and the school to which General Lee went is now a big college.

In those days there was no railroad to Lexington, so you may guess how the General went there.

He rode on Traveler.

As he went along the road, mile after mile, he would now and then meet one of his old soldiers. The man would look first at the white horse; then he would look at the gray-bearded rider. Then he would take off his hat. He was so glad to see "Marse Robert" and Traveler once more!

At last General Lee reached Lexington. There he and Traveler both lived after that, and there they both died.

# PLANTING A TREE

## (For Arbor Day)

Once a great man went on a long, long journey. He went clear around the world! When he was about halfway around he planted a tree. I am going to tell you about that tree.

But you don't know who the great man was, do you? I must tell you his name first.

His name was Grant. Most people call him General Grant. He was a general and he was also President of the United States for eight years.

It was after General Grant had been President that he made his long trip around the world. He was away three years on that trip. Because he was such a famous man everybody was glad to see him and wanted to shake hands with him. So it took him a long time to get around.

He went from place to place, from one country to another. When he was about halfway around the world he came to a country called Japan. It was in Japan that he planted the tree that I am telling you about.

The people of Japan love trees. They love cherry trees best, and they plant a great many cherry trees. In the spring of the year all the cherry trees are white with blossoms and are very beautiful.

I do not know whether it was a cherry tree that General Grant planted in Japan but he planted a tree of some kind and it is still growing there to-day.

It is in a beautiful park, with many other trees. The park is in a large city. The people of the city take good care of the tree, and when somebody from our country goes there on a visit they take him out to the park and say:

"This is the tree that General Grant planted."

They also put pictures of the tree on post cards and sell them to visitors. Once in a while somebody who is traveling around the world now buys one of these cards and sends it to a friend in America.

Every spring we have a day called Arbor Day. Arbor Day is Tree Day. On Arbor Day we plant trees. To-day is Arbor Day, and we are going to plant a tree.

Let us plant a tree whenever we can. Trees make the world beautiful; they make people happy.

> There's a pretty tree,
> So far across the sea,
> Growing there,
> Strong and fair,
> Far across the sea.

Would you like to see
How quick the General's tree
   Grows a span,
   In Japan,
Far across the sea?

Let us plant a tree;
'Twill grow for you and me
   In the sun,
   Like the one
Far across the sea!

Let us go now and plant our tree; but do not forget the little story about General Grant and the tree he planted on the other side of the world.

# YELLOW KING CORN

Let us talk to-day about King Corn. We call him Yellow King Corn; but sometimes King Corn is white, and once in a while he is red.

How many of you have seen an ear of white corn? How many have seen a red ear?

Long ago when the white people came to this country they found King Corn among the Indians. The Indians were growing corn. They taught the white men how to do it, and soon the white men were growing corn, too.

Then the white men carried King Corn across the sea. Now King Corn is found in many, many lands.

The Indians told a story about King Corn. This is the story.

Once an Indian boy went out into the forest. He went into the forest to fast and to live alone. He built a little wigwam and painted his face black. Then he lay down in the wigwam to rest, for he was very tired.

As he lay in the wigwam he gazed up at the blue sky. All the time he was praying to the Master of Life. He prayed not for himself, but for his people. He said:

Yellow King Corn

"O Master of Life, send me a gift for my people! O Master of Life, send me a gift for my people!"

Then the Indian boy saw some one coming. It was a young man, a beautiful young man. He came down from heaven. He wore a green coat and he had green plumes on his head.

The young man said to the Indian boy, "You must wrestle with me. You must wrestle with me and throw me on the ground. This is the only way you can get a gift for your people."

The Indian boy was weak and faint, but he wanted a gift for his people. So he got up and began to wrestle with the beautiful young man.

They wrestled and they wrestled, but neither one could throw the other. After a while the beautiful young man went away, but he said, "I'll come back to-morrow."

When he returned the next day he and the Indian boy wrestled again. They wrestled and they wrestled, but neither one could throw the other.

On the third day it was the same way; but when the beautiful young man went away on the third day he said to the Indian boy:

"To-morrow you will throw me and win a gift for your people."

And sure enough it was so. On the fourth day the Indian boy wrestled again with the beautiful young man and threw him.

After the Indian boy had thrown the young man on

the ground he stripped off the young man's beautiful, green coat. Then he buried him in the soft, fresh ground.

Once in a while the Indian boy went back to the place where he had buried the beautiful young man, to pull up the grass and weeds and keep them from growing on the grave.

It was not long till the Indian boy saw the young man's green plumes waving over the grave. When autumn came the place was covered with tall stalks of corn, and on the stalks were big yellow ears.

Then the Indian boy was happy and took the corn home. He gave it to his people. It was the gift for which he had prayed to the Master of Life.

This is the story of King Corn that the Indians told.

King Corn is very useful. He helps man and beast in more than a hundred different ways.

Corn, as you know, is good for making cakes and bread. Hominy is also made from corn. The Indians used to make hominy. The stalks and leaves of corn make good food for cattle and sheep. Some parts of corn stalks are used for making paper. Corn cobs are good for fuel. Corn husks are fine for making rugs and baskets.

And we must not forget popcorn balls! The inside of the popcorn grains is snowy white. When the grains pop they turn inside out and look like flakes of snow. Then when we stick them together the balls look like snowballs. But they are better to eat than snowballs.

We could hardly get along without King Corn, could we? We think of him a great deal at Thanksgiving time.

# WHITE KING COTTON

To-day I am going to talk with you about King Cotton; but first I shall tell you a little story about a young man who had wheels in his head.

This young man's name was Samuel, and he lived in England at first. His full name was Samuel Slater.

Samuel Slater worked in a cotton mill. He saw the wheels go round every day; he heard the big machines buzz and rattle. He saw the long white threads come out, and he saw the threads woven into strong white cloth.

And Samuel Slater not only saw and heard; he also took hold and helped. As I said, he worked in a cotton mill.

And there was something else that he did: he thought in a cotton mill. All that noise and bustle couldn't keep him from thinking. The cotton mill was his lesson. He studied the cotton mill every day, and he learned his lesson.

One day Samuel Slater heard a piece of news that caused him to open his eyes. It had come across the sea—it was a piece of news from this country, from America, this land of ours.

And this is the bit of news that Samuel Slater heard:

"The people in America want a new cotton mill. They want a cotton mill like the mills in England."

What do you think Samuel Slater said? He said: "I'm going to America and build a cotton mill."

And that is just what he did. He got on a ship, came over to this country, and built a new cotton mill like the ones in England.

But the king of England would not let anybody carry cotton machines out of England. He would not even allow a picture of a cotton machine to be carried out.

So Samuel Slater had to go to work, when he got over here, and make his own machines. He had no pictures to look at—he had no books to read. The king of England wouldn't let him bring any.

So he just made the machines from memory. He built the whole mill from the pictures in his mind. This is the reason why I spoke of him as having wheels in his head.

In England he had studied while he worked. The mill was his lesson. He had learned his lesson. Then he was able to come over here and build a mill from memory.

Samuel Slater made a great deal of money. He also helped our people to have plenty of cotton goods. And he helped to make cotton king.

Cotton grows in many parts of the world, but more

grows in our country than anywhere else. In the South, where the sun shines warm, cotton grows best. King Cotton likes a warm day.

A big cotton field in bloom is very beautiful. The green buds burst open white. The branches of the plants are full of buds and are close together. Then the field of cotton looks like a forest of little trees covered with snow. But when the sun shines this snow doesn't melt. King Cotton loves a warm day.

Men and women, boys and girls, then go into the cotton field with large bags and baskets. They pick off the white bunches of cotton and carry them away. Then the seeds are taken out and the white cotton is tied up in big bundles called bales.

Next the bales are put on the cars or on a ship and taken to a mill, or factory. There the cotton is spun into threads and the threads are woven into cloth. Much of our nice soft clothing is made of cotton.

Some day I'll tell you about Eli Whitney. He was another young man who had wheels in his head. He also helped to make cotton king.

Here is an old rhyme about King Cotton:

> Old Cotton will pleasantly reign
>    When other kings painfully fall,
> And ever and ever remain
>    The mightiest monarch of all.

# BLACK KING COAL

Long, long ago King Coal stuffed a lot of sunshine into his pocket and hid in some deep, dark caves.

King Coal was not black in those days, but he stayed in the deep, dark caves so long that he turned black—just as black as a crow.

And the sunshine was in the dark so long that it forgot how to smile! All its pretty smiles turned into black pictures, and it grew as black and ugly as old King Coal.

Then King Coal waited to see what would happen. He was down in the caves so deep he didn't think that anybody could find him. And every year he went down a little deeper.

"Now, then," whispered old King Coal, "I'm pretty safe. Nobody can find me away down here in the dark!"

But somebody did find him. One day some men with picks and shovels went to one of his caves and dug him out. I mean, they dug out a piece of him. Maybe it was just one of his toes, or the tip of his nose, or a button off of his old black coat. King Coal is so big that it takes no end of work to dig him out—all of him—and the job is not finished yet.

For a long time King Coal wouldn't tell what he had done with the sunshine. He wouldn't say a word—he wouldn't do a thing.

But at last somebody said: "Let's warm him up! Maybe he'll do something or say something when he gets warm."

So they put King Coal in the fire to warm him up. And sure enough! as he grew warmer and warmer, and hotter and hotter, he began to do the most wonderful things!

He began to make the water boil. He made the whole house warm. He heated iron for the blacksmith, and made steam for the engine on the railroad. He began to push big ships up the rivers and across the ocean; and in a little while he was making all the wheels in a factory go buzz! buzz! buzz!

King Coal became so useful to everybody that people learned to like him, even though he was black and dirty; even though he had stolen the sunshine.

And now—this is the most wonderful part of my story—when King Coal got red-hot he told what he had done with the sunshine. He just couldn't help it, I guess; for when he grew red-hot the sunshine jumped out of his pocket and smiled at everybody in the room!

And everybody was so glad that the sunshine had found its smile again.

Now King Coal is everybody's good friend. He is black and dirty and greasy—he just can't help it—he was down in the deep, dark caves so long; but everybody is glad to see him and everybody is glad to have him around.

And every time that King Coal gets red-hot the sunshine jumps out of his pocket and smiles. In fact, a good many people watch the coal fire just to see whether King Coal himself doesn't smile.

# STRONG KING IRON

Have you ever seen a man chop down a tree? A wood-chopper has a long, smooth stick, and on the end of it is a sharp steel ax.

When men first began to chop down trees, long ago, they used stone axes. Stone axes were very dull; so it took a long time to cut down a tree with a stone ax.

After a while people began to make axes and knives of copper. The copper knives and axes were better than the stone ones, but still they were not very good.

Then somebody found some iron and made an ax of iron. It was much better than the axes of stone and of copper. Finally, somebody else learned how to make the iron very hard. This hard iron was called steel. Then the axes of steel cut best of all.

Every ax you see nowadays is made of this hard iron, called steel. It does not take long to cut down a tree with a sharp steel ax.

Iron is used for so many things that we could hardly get along without it. Did you ever have a pair of roller-skates? They were made largely of iron. Did you ever ride in an automobile? Automobiles are made chiefly of iron.

The range in the kitchen, the furnace in the cellar, the weights in the windows, the nails in the floor, are all made of iron. Even ships that cross the sea, cars on the railroad, and flying machines that shoot through the air are made largely of iron.

Do you not think that we may call iron king? And because iron is so strong, do you not think we may call him Strong King Iron?

Strong King Iron reaches his arms across wide rivers and makes bridges for us. He stands up in the sky and holds up our tallest and heaviest buildings. He rolls himself up into a big cannon and shoots twenty miles. Now he hides in your coat as a needle or a pin and sticks your finger. He stretches himself out on the railroad track and carries all the trolley cars and trains. He hangs himself up on the telegraph and telephone poles and carries our messages around the world.

He is every carpenter's saw, every blacksmith's hammer, every farmer's plow, every miner's pick, every gardener's hoe, every soldier's sword, every lady's needle, and every boy's knife.

King Iron is very old. Perhaps this is the reason that he is gray. But he has not always been king. As I told you, people had to use stone and copper for a long time because they did not know King Iron.

But iron has been king for many, many years. In times of peace he makes the world happy; in times of war he makes it very sad. But all the time the world goes much faster than it did before iron became king; for King Iron has put the world on wheels.

# HEAVY KING GOLD

Come and hear this little story about Heavy King Gold.

Iron is strong and heavy, and lead is heavier than iron. Do you know how heavy lead is? But gold is heavier than iron; gold is heavier than lead; so we call gold "Heavy King Gold."

Perhaps you wonder how there can be so many kings. We have talked about Yellow King Corn, about White King Cotton, about Black King Coal, about Strong King Iron; and now we are talking about Heavy King Gold.

Well, there always have been many kings in the world. One king rules here, another king rules there, and other kings rule in other places.

So it is with these kings of whom we speak. King Corn rules on the farms; King Cotton rules in the factories; King Coal rules in the furnaces; King Iron rules in the shops; and King Gold rules in the banks.

One day a man in California was digging a big ditch. It was at a sawmill, and he was digging the ditch to carry water away from the sawmill. Many sawmills are run by water power; and the big ditch that carries the water is called a race.

This man, when the race was dug, stood by it watching the water run through. The water was clear and he could see the sand and pebbles at the bottom of the race.

All at once the man saw something bright and shining among the pebbles. He got down into the race, put his hand into the water, and took up the shining thing. It was about as big as a pea, and it was heavy! It wasn't clay, it wasn't copper, and it wasn't silver. The man thought it might be gold, but he wasn't certain. He knew that not everything is gold that glitters.

He took the heavy shining thing and laid it on a stone. Then he took another stone and pounded it. The heavy shining thing did not break. It was soft and it flattened out as he hammered it.

By this time the man could hardly stand still. He was excited. He looked into the water and found some more heavy shining things. "Can this be gold?" he said to himself. Then he was excited more than ever. He put some of the heavy shining things into his pocket, jumped on his horse, and rode forty miles. He wanted to find out what he had. If he had found gold he wanted to know it; for it is a great thing to find gold.

Sure enough, the heavy shining things were gold. The man jumped on his horse again, rode back forty miles to the sawmill, and began to dig. In a few days men were digging all around that sawmill as fast as they could. They all wanted gold. Gold was king.

It was not long till people were going to California from all directions. They had heard that gold was there.

Gold was king. King Gold was calling them.

And this is the story of King Gold all over the world. Wherever King Gold is thought to be, there men run to find him. He weighs heavier and he calls louder than any of the other kings. He has his throne in the banks—the banks are his palaces—but he is a king everywhere.

# CHUCKY JACK AND HIS HORSE

"Chucky Jack" was a brave man who lived long ago— over a hundred years ago. He was born in Virginia, but he is buried in Tennessee. Most of his lifetime he lived in Tennessee.

I know that you are wondering why this man had such a funny name—"Chucky Jack." Isn't it a funny name? Well, I'll tell you why he was called "Chucky Jack."

His real name was John, but his friends liked nicknames, so they called him Jack. He lived near a beautiful river. The river is called the Nollichucky. I imagine the river was named by the Indians.

Now you see, because John was Jack, and because he lived near the Nollichucky River, he was called "Nollichucky Jack." That was his nickname.

But people also like short names. "Nollichucky Jack" was too long. The hunters of Tennessee did not always have time to say "Nollichucky Jack," so they cut off the first part and just said "Chucky Jack."

Now you see how it was, don't you?

But I promised to tell you about Chucky Jack and his horse.

Chucky Jack had more than one horse, but he had one that he liked best of all. She could run faster than any of the others. In fact, it is said that she could run faster than any other horse in Tennessee.

In those days, when Chucky Jack often had to go after bad Indians, he needed a horse that could run fast.

One time Chucky Jack was arrested. He was taken to town and was in danger of being put in jail. Some of his friends were afraid that he might be hanged.

Now if Chucky Jack had been a bad man he ought to have been put in jail; but he wasn't a bad man. Most people were certain that he ought not to have been arrested.

So his friends went to town to help him. They did not know just what to do, because they did not want to hurt anybody.

At last they thought of a plan. They got Chucky Jack's horse—the one that could run so fast—and led her to town. They put a bridle and a saddle on her and let her stand right in front of the courthouse door. When Chucky Jack looked out he saw his horse. He knew her, of course. And he also knew that his friends had brought her there.

Then one of his friends, whose name was Cosby, came walking into the courthouse. He went right straight up to the judge and began talking with him. He raised his hand and talked so loud that everybody looked and listened.

Just at that moment, when everybody was looking

at Cosby, Chucky Jack jumped up, ran out of the courthouse, and leaped on his horse. As soon as he touched the saddle his horse started off as fast as she could run. She ran out of the town, into the woods, and into the mountains. She kept on running till she carried Chucky Jack safely home.

*Chucky Jack Riding Home*

# DAVY CROCKETT
# AND THE BEARS

Did you ever hear of Davy Crockett? He was a great bear hunter. He was out in the woods so much of his time that he learned all about bears.

He knew what bears like to eat. He knew where they like to sleep. Often he would look into a cave in the rocks or into a hole in a big hollow tree and find a bear.

Sometimes he would find a tree with scratches on it, made by a bear's sharp claws. By looking at the scratches Davy Crockett could tell whether the bear had climbed up the tree or down.

At one time Crockett owned eight big dogs. These dogs went with him and helped him to hunt bears. Sometimes when the dogs found a bear and held him fast with their sharp teeth, Crockett would go right up to the bear and kill him with his big knife.

If the bear were up in a tree he would shoot him with his rifle. Whenever the rifle cracked the bear would come tumbling down; for Davy Crockett was a dead shot. When he took aim and pulled the trigger he hardly ever missed.

When bears are fat their meat is good to eat. Davy Crockett and his neighbors liked bear meat and often used it instead of beef or pork.

All of his neighbors knew that Crockett was a good bear hunter, so they were always anxious for him to go along when they went out to kill bears.

One time when one of his neighbors was out of meat he asked Crockett to go hunting with him. They went out into the woods and stayed two weeks. By that time they had killed fourteen bears. Then, you may be sure, the man and his family had plenty of meat for a long time.

At another time Crockett saw a poor man who was working very hard. The man looked pale and sick. He said that he and his family had no meat to eat. Crockett said, "Come along with me, let's kill some bears."

They took their guns and went out into the forest. Before night they had four bears, and by the end of the week they had killed thirteen more. They divided the meat and the poor man had enough to last him and his family a year.

One night when Crockett was out hunting bears he got wet in wading through a river and came near freezing to death, for it was cold. It was so dark that he could not find his way back to camp. He tried to make a fire, but the wood did not burn enough to make him warm.

At last he found a way to make him warm, but you could never guess what he did. Do you want to know?

Well, this is what he did. He found a tree that was tall and smooth. He climbed up this tree, then locked his arms and legs around it and slid down. He slid down fast.

Then he climbed up again and slid down again in the same way. This he kept up until daylight, and thus he kept from freezing to death.

In one month this great hunter killed forty-seven bears; and in one year he killed one hundred and five. At the same time he did many other things besides hunt bears.

## PART TWO

# ALEXANDER THE GREAT

About two thousand years ago a boy became a king. His name was Alexander, and he was such a great king that he is called Alexander the Great.

Alexander's father was a king—a great king, too,—and did many wonderful things. One day Alexander was sad, and when somebody asked him what was the matter he replied:

"I'm afraid that my father will do everything and leave nothing for me to do!"

Alexander wanted to be a soldier, like his father, but he also loved books. He had a good teacher and learned his lessons well. Every night when Alexander went to bed he would take his sword and his book and put them under his pillow.

The Alexander story that I like best is about Alexander and Bucephalus.

Bucephalus was a horse. When Alexander was a boy Bucephalus was a colt. Bucephalus was very wild—nobody could ride him or tame him, it seemed.

One day when some strong men were trying to ride Bucephalus Alexander stood by and watched them. Whenever one of the men would try to mount him Bucephalus would rear up on his hind feet and jump around so much that the man had no chance at all.

At last the men started to lead the horse away. They thought he never would be fit to ride.

Alexander exclaimed: "What a pity to lose such a good horse!"

Nobody paid any attention to him.

Then Alexander cried out again: "What a pity to lose such a good horse!"

When he had said this two or three times his father heard him and spoke to him rather sharply:

"Do you think that you know more about that horse than the men do?"

"I can manage him," the boy replied, "if you will only let me try."

Then everybody laughed. They thought that the boy did not know what he was talking about.

But at last they brought the horse back and let Alexander take hold of the bridle.

The first thing Alexander did was to turn Bucephalus around.

Why do you suppose he did that?

This is the reason why he did it. Alexander had noticed that Bucephalus was frightened by his own

# Alexander the Great

shadow; so he turned him around, with his face toward the sun, so he could not see his shadow.

Then Alexander jumped on the horse's back. He did not whip him or kick him, but handled him gently till he became quiet. Then he let him go faster and faster till Bucephalus was running with all his might.

All this time Alexander's father and his friends were watching. They were much afraid that Bucephalus would throw the boy off.

But Alexander stuck on. He let the horse run straight ahead for half a mile or so, then he turned him around and came riding back at full speed.

When Alexander jumped off his father kissed him and said:

"My son, go find a kingdom for yourself; my kingdom is too small for you."

From that day on Bucephalus and Alexander were good friends. Bucephalus proved to be the best kind of horse and he carried his master safely for many a day. When Alexander wanted to cross a river Bucephalus took him over. When Alexander rode into battle he was mounted on Bucephalus. When Alexander set out to conquer the world Bucephalus carried him.

After Bucephalus had carried Alexander for thousands of miles, through many lands, he died far away from home. Alexander buried him and named a city after him.

# CHARLES THE GREAT

To-day I am going to tell you about a king whose name was Charles. He is called Charles the Great.

What do you think this great king called himself? He called himself David. This was because he often read in the Bible about King David and thought that King David was a great man.

In many ways Charles the Great was like King David. He was a brave soldier; he liked to study books; he loved music; and he was anxious to build schools and churches.

King Charles was tall and strong. He could ride a horse all day and was fond of hunting. He could speak and read well, but he never learned to write well.

What do you think was the reason why King Charles never learned to write well?

It was not because he didn't try. He tried hard. He would put a pencil and tablet under his pillow at night, and if he could not sleep he would sit up in bed and practice writing. He tried just as hard as he could to learn how to write.

The trouble was that he had not begun when he was a boy. He had not begun to write till he was a grown man. By that time his fingers were hard and stiff. By that time they fitted around the thick handle of a sword much better than they did around the slender staff of a pen.

One Christmas day King Charles was in a large church in a great city. As he was kneeling down praying the pastor (bishop) of the church came up and put a splendid crown on his head.

Charles was a king before that time, and had a king's crown; but after the day when the bishop gave him another crown he was called emperor as well as king.

As I have already told you, Charles the Great was anxious to build schools and churches. A number of the schools in his kingdom were in churches, and the pastors of the churches were the teachers.

Charles had a great school in his palace. For this school he got the best teachers he could find. He went to many places looking for good teachers, and whenever he found one that was very good he invited him to his palace.

In King Charles's palace school were grown-up men as well as boys. There were perhaps some women, too, and a few girls.

One day King Charles found out that the rich boys in his school were not studying as well as the poor boys, and he decided to give the lazy fellows a lesson himself.

He told the poor boys to sit in the right-hand side of the room. They were the sheep. He made the rich boys sit in the left-hand side of the room. They were the goats.

Then he praised the poor boys for their good work and declared that he was pleased with them; but he gave the rich boys a severe scolding. He finished by saying to them:

"If you want any more favors from me you will have to go to work and get your lessons."

Don't you think that was a pretty good thing for a king to say to a lot of lazy boys?

# ALFRED THE GREAT

Once there was in England a good king named Alfred. He was so brave and wise and did so many fine things for his people that he is always called Alfred the Great.

When Alfred was a little boy his mother had a nice book. It was a copy of the Bible. She also had five sons, Alfred being the youngest. One day she called the five boys to her and showed them the nice book. She said:

"I'll give this book to the one of you that learns first to read it."

The five young princes began to study hard. They studied one reading lesson after another, as fast as they could. The Bible was a fine prize, and each one of them was anxious to win it.

Not very long afterwards one of the boys came to his mother and said, "Mother, I believe that I can read the book now." And sure enough, when she gave him a test, he could read it; and he received it as a prize.

Now, which of the five princes do you think it was who won the prize?

Yes, it was Alfred, the youngest of the five. He won the beautiful book, and he loved books all his life.

While Alfred was king the Danes were fighting his people—the English. The Danes were strong, fierce people who came in boats from another country. They wanted to live in England, and they tried to rob and kill Alfred's people.

*Alfred Learning To Read*

King Alfred had a hard time fighting the Danes, but at last he beat them in one or two battles and made them stay in one part of the country by themselves. He drew a long line between his people and the Danes and would not allow the Danes to cross the line.

Alfred trained his men to be good soldiers. At the same time he allowed some of them to stay on their farms all the time in order that plenty of food might be produced for everybody.

King Alfred also had his men build ships. In time of war the ships were used to carry soldiers, and all the time they were used to carry food and other things that the people needed.

And all his life, as I have told you, Alfred the Great loved books. He loved books so much that he wanted all of his people to have books, and he wanted every boy (maybe every girl, too) to learn to read.

So King Alfred built schoolhouses and hired schoolteachers. He gathered together many good books and many good teachers. But as long as he lived there was one book that he always loved best: it was the Bible—the book he had first learned to read.

# PETER THE GREAT

About two hundred years ago King Peter lived in Russia. Russia is a large country on the other side of the ocean. King Peter was fierce and cruel, but he also was able and wide awake. He did so much to help Russia that he is called Peter the Great.

Peter was crowned king when he was only ten years old. He was not a real king then—he was just a bad, noisy boy. He did not go to school much and so did not know much.

But after a while Peter began to study more and to learn more. How do you think he did it? Instead of reading in books about places and things, he went to see them. For example, when he wanted to know how to build ships he went to Holland. In Holland the people were first-class ship-builders.

So to Holland Peter went. He did not tell anybody, though, that he was a king. He put on a suit of old clothes, a pair of coarse shoes, went to the gate of the shipyard, and said:

"Won't you give me a job? I want to learn how to build ships."

The boss said: "I can't pay you much at first, but if you'll behave yourself and work hard I'll give you a job."

So Peter went to work. He sawed logs till his back ached. He chopped and hammered till he rubbed blisters on his hands. He got tired and thirsty, but he stuck to his job. All the time he kept his eyes open. He said to himself, "This is pretty hard work for a king, but I'm learning to build ships."

After Peter had learned a good deal about ship-building he left Holland. He shook hands with the other workmen and said, "Good-by"; but even then he did not tell them that he was a king.

Peter then went to other countries to see what he could learn; and at some places he let the people know who he was. Whenever he saw anything new he was just like a boy—he would ask all sorts of questions about it and would try to take it apart. He wanted to see how it worked and what it looked like on the inside.

After Peter the Great had traveled around a great deal himself he made other young men of Russia do the same thing, in order that they, too, might learn how other nations did things, and might return to Russia able to teach their own people.

Wherever Peter found a good teacher—in Holland, in England, in Germany—he would ask him to go to Russia. Wherever he found a good doctor he would say to him, "Come to Russia." Wherever he found a man who could build a house or a bridge better than others it was the same thing—"Come to Russia."

Peter wanted men in Russia who could do things and could do them well. All his life he was on the lookout for them. He wanted the very best men and the very best things for Russia.

So we call him Peter the Great, even if he had a bad temper and sometimes did cruel things. He had a keen eye, and kept it open. He had a skillful hand, and used it. He had a wise head, and proved it. And he loved Russia.

# THE BOY WHO DREAMED

Once there was a boy who was always dreaming. He dreamed that he saw a sheaf of wheat stand up, and that he then saw eleven other sheaves stand up around it and bow to it. He dreamed that he saw the sun and the moon and the stars all making bows to him.

He told one of his dreams to his father. His father thought it was all very foolish, and told him not to be dreaming so much. When he told his dreams to his brothers they became angry. You see there were eleven of them, and when Joseph (that was the boy's name) told about the eleven sheaves his brothers thought he was dreaming about them. They never did like him, anyhow.

One day Joseph's brothers did a very wicked thing. They took him and sold him to some strangers. These strangers were merchants and they carried Joseph with them into another country. In that country, which is called Egypt, Joseph was kept many, many years. All the time his father and mother did not know where he was.

At first Joseph had a hard time in Egypt. He was a slave and was sometimes mistreated. Once he was put into prison and kept there a long time.

Later Joseph became a great man. He was loved by the king and was given a fine place in the king's palace. The king had had a wonderful dream and Joseph had told him what it meant. That was the reason why the king loved him and made him a great man. You see Joseph still had a great deal to do with dreams.

After Joseph had become a great man in Egypt his brothers at home began to have a hard time. Their crops did not grow and their cattle did not thrive. They had very little to eat. There was a famine one year, a famine the next year, and so on for seven years.

Now in Egypt there was plenty to eat, in spite of the hard times. Joseph and the king had managed things so well that the people in Egypt had enough to eat and some to spare. In fact, the Egyptians sold a great deal of food to the people of other countries.

And now, what do you think? Joseph's brothers went to Egypt to buy food! They had to buy it of Joseph, for he had charge of the king's storehouse.

Joseph had changed so much that his brothers did not know him, but he knew them. He might have put them in jail, but he didn't do it. He sold them food and after a long time he told them who he was. They were very much surprised and were terribly frightened; but Joseph did not hurt them. He believed in doing a good turn for a bad one.

After this Joseph's father and all his brothers went to Egypt to live. Joseph and the king picked them out good farms and rich pasture fields near the river—the big river Nile. If it had not been for Joseph there is no telling what would have become of his father, of his brothers, or of their children. The boy who was a great dreamer turned out to be a man who was a great doer.

Now, in closing this story, let me tell you a secret about Joseph. He did most of his dreaming in the daytime, when he was wide awake. I mean just this: He was a boy who kept his eyes open and could see what ought to be done. He saw things, then he went to work to do things. This is the reason his dreams always counted for so much.

# THE SHEPHERD BOY
# AND THE GIANT

One day, long ago, two armies were just ready to fight. In one army was King Saul, who was very tall and strong. He was a head taller than any man in his army.

But in the other army was a giant, who was much taller and stronger than King Saul. If the giant had stood up straight and held out his arm, King Saul could have stood right under it.

What do you think the giant did?

When the armies were just ready to fight the giant walked out in front and shouted, "Don't fight!"

Then he shouted to King Saul and said:

"Pick out your best man and send him over here. Let him fight me. If he shall kill me, all of my army will serve you; if I kill him, then all of your army must serve us."

That sounded fair, didn't it? But the trouble was, nobody in King Saul's army was able to fight the giant. Even King Saul himself, tall and strong as he was, was no match for the giant. The giant knew this. So did King Saul. Everybody knew this. Every big man in Saul's army was afraid of the giant.

But just then somebody came up who was not afraid of the giant. It was a shepherd boy. His home was at Bethlehem, a little town up in the mountains, fifteen miles away. He had run down to see his big brothers, who were in Saul's army.

The shepherd boy said, "Who is this giant? What will King Saul give me to kill him?"

This made one of his big brothers very angry and he said:

"What are you doing here, anyhow? You had better be at home, looking after those sheep."

But the shepherd boy kept on talking until King Saul heard what he said; and the king finally said:

"We'll give you a chance at the giant. We'll see whether you can do what you say."

Then the shepherd boy went out to fight the giant. The giant had a long spear and a big sword. He also had a man to carry a large shield in front of him.

What do you think the shepherd boy had? King Saul offered him a sword and a lot of other things, but he wouldn't take them. He just took his sling in one hand and his sheep stick in the other.

Do you all know what a sling is? How many of you have seen a sling? It is a piece of leather with strings to it, used for throwing stones. If one of you boys will make a sling and bring it to school to-morrow, we'll all take a look at it.

# The Shepherd Boy and the Giant

Now this shepherd boy was a fine slinger. He had used a sling so much that he could hit the mark nearly every time. And when he threw a stone with his sling it just whizzed—it flew almost like a bullet.

This time he picked up five good stones and put them into his pocket. He was so eager to meet the giant that he ran. When he got close enough he stopped, put a stone into his sling, whirled it around his head, and let it fly. The stone flew just above the giant's shield and struck him right in the forehead. He fell to the ground and in a few minutes he was dead. But the shepherd boy took no chances. He ran up, seized the giant's own sword, and cut off his head.

How many of you know what this shepherd boy's name was? Yes, it was David; and the giant's name was—Goliath.

This is a Bible story. David said that he was able to kill the giant because God helped him.

# THE FIRST CHRISTMAS GIFT

Do you know the story about the first Christmas gift? I'll tell you the story, but first I am going to tell you about three other Christmas gifts.

Three beautiful Christmas gifts were given to a baby boy, nearly two thousand years ago. He was just a little baby that Christmas, and he was in a stable.

I'm sure you think that a stable is an odd place for a little baby to be, so I'll tell you why this baby was in a stable.

His parents were away from home. They were at a town called Bethlehem. There was no room for them in the hotel, so they had to find lodging somewhere else. They looked here and there, but the only place they could find was a corner in a stable. There they had to stay for several days. That is the reason why this baby received his gifts in a stable.

This baby boy's Christmas gifts were carried to him by some grown-up men. They were wise men. The wise men traveled a long, long way to get to Bethlehem. They had never seen the little child, and they did not know just where he was; but they were led to him by a bright star.

And they knew that the baby boy was a king!

As they went along the road they could not always see the star. Once in a while they would ask somebody where the little king was. They would say:

"Where is he that is born King of the Jews? for we have seen his star in the East, and are come to worship him."

But for a long time nobody could tell them where the baby king was.

After a while they came to a city that is only five or six miles from Bethlehem. There they stopped and asked the question again:

"Where is he that is born King of the Jews? for we have seen his star in the East, and are come to worship him."

And somebody said, "In Bethlehem."

Then the wise men set out for Bethlehem, and as soon as they did that they saw the star again. It showed them just where to go.

When the wise men saw the baby king they bowed down low before him and worshiped him. Then they gave him the three gifts that they had brought for him.

And what do you think those three gifts were?

One was gold. I do not know how much gold was in the gift, or just what the shape of it was; but it was gold—beautiful, precious, shining gold.

Another gift was frankincense. This is something that has a very sweet odor. It is also very precious perhaps just as precious as gold.

The third gift was myrrh. Myrrh also has a sweet odor and it is a good medicine. It is good to heal sick people and make them well.

All these gifts were very precious. They were just the kind of gifts for a king. The wise men brought them to little King Jesus.

I have told you about those three Christmas gifts. Now I must tell you about the first Christmas gift.

King Jesus himself was the first Christmas gift. God gave him to the world to bless the world, and to make little children happy every Christmas.

> To a King
> Wise men bring
> Treasures from afar;
> To his bed
> They are led
> By a wondrous star.
>
> Three gifts fair,
> Rich and rare,
> They with joy unfold
> At his feet:
> Incense sweet,
> Myrrh, and shining gold!
>
> It was meet,
> At his feet,
> With rich gifts to fall,
> For the King
> Love did bring,
> The first, best gift of all.

# EASTER CANDLES

Have you ever seen a candle as tall as a tree? I'm going to tell you about one.

In the city of Durham, in England, is a grand old cathedral. Do you know what a cathedral is? It is a big church.

There are many big churches, called cathedrals, in England; but the cathedral at Durham is one of the largest and one of the finest. It stands on a high bank, beside a river; and the river is often so still and clear that you can see a beautiful picture of the cathedral in the water.

But I started to tell you about a candle as tall as a tree. Well, I'll get to that in a moment.

Many years ago there was such a candle in the Cathedral of Durham every Easter. It stood on a huge candlestick of brass. The candlestick was as tall as a little tree, and when the big wax candle was put into it the candlestick and the candle together were as tall as a large tree.

But just think of it! That big candlestick, with the long candle on top of it, as tall as a tree, stood inside the church! What a large church Durham Cathedral must be!

And how do you suppose anybody ever got up to the top of that candle to light it? There was no man tall enough to reach up. And the wax candle was too slippery for any one to climb it.

Maybe you think that the man who lighted that tall candle went up on a ladder, but he didn't. I don't believe that you ever would guess how he did it, so I'll tell you.

He did it this way. He went upstairs and reached down through a hole in the ceiling. He probably put the fire on the end of a long stick; then he could reach down far enough to touch the tip of the wick. Then the great candle would begin to burn. What a light it must have made!

Now, if I tell you about the branches of that big candle you will think that it was like a tree sure enough.

It had four long branches. One branch extended towards the north, another towards the south; a third extended towards the east, and a fourth towards the west.

When the big candle and its four branches were all lighted it must have looked somewhat like the moon with four big stars around it.

That candle was so big that it did not all burn up at Easter. So it was left standing in the church for fifty days after Easter, and at every service it was lighted.

At the end of the fifty days there would still be some of the candle left. It was then taken down and made into a great number of little candles, and those candles were given to the poor people who lived near the cathedral.

So that wonderful Easter candle, as tall as a tree, first made a great light; then it made many little lights. At Easter all the people could go to the church and see the great light; afterwards many of them could carry a candle home and have a light there.

At other great churches in England were other large Easter candles; but I am told that the one at Durham Cathedral was the largest of them all.

# HOW A KING GOT
# OUT OF PRISON

Perhaps you wonder how a king got into prison. It is not often that a king is in prison, but it is so once in a while. Long ago it was so oftener than it is nowadays.

The king I am going to tell you about was King Richard. He was king of England many, many years ago.

One time King Richard was far away from home. He had been away from home a long time and was anxious to get back. He was traveling as fast as he could, but one day he had to pass near the castle of Duke Leopold. Duke Leopold did not like King Richard, so he sent some of his men to capture him.

It must have taken a number of men to do this, for King Richard was very brave and very strong. He was so brave and strong that people called him Richard the Lion-Heart.

But in spite of all his courage and in spite of all his strength King Richard was captured by the Duke's men and was put in prison. The Duke said he would keep him in prison until somebody paid a large sum of money to get him out.

The worst of it was that King Richard's friends in England did not know what had become of him. They waited and waited for him to come home, but he did not come. Then they wondered and wondered where he was.

Among King Richard's friends was a young man named Blondel. Blondel could make poetry and sing songs. King Richard liked to hear him sing, and sometimes he and Blondel sang together. Blondel said, "I am going to find King Richard."

So he set out and journeyed far and wide. He would ask this man and that man about King Richard, but nobody could tell him where the king was. Then he would go on till he met another man.

"Have you seen King Richard?" he would ask.

The man would answer, "No."

"Do you know where he is?"

"No."

How tired poor Blondel must have been! He was tired and sad. He began to fear that he never would find King Richard.

But he kept on trying.

One day Blondel saw a great castle. The walls were high and strong, and soldiers guarded the gates. Blondel could not get in, and nobody would tell him anything about his master, King Richard.

After a while Blondel began to sing. He sang a song that he and Richard had made. Nobody but he and the king knew that song. He sang the first part of the song, then stopped and listened.

What do you think? He heard somebody in the castle begin to sing. A man in the castle was singing the next part of the same song!

Then Blondel knew that King Richard was in the castle. Nobody else knew that song! Nobody else had such a voice!

But Blondel did not have as much money as Duke Leopold wanted; so back to England he went. He met the king's brother John, but John did not like Richard and would not help much. Then he went to see King Richard's mother. She helped, you may be sure. After a while

*Blondel at the Castle*

86

they had as much money as the Duke demanded, and he let King Richard out.

But King Richard always said he did not believe that he ever would have gotten out of prison if it had not been for Blondel's song.

# THE RED VELVET CLOAK

Have you ever seen a velvet cloak? Cloaks of velvet are very soft and beautiful, and they cost a great deal of money.

One day a young man in the city of London had on a handsome red velvet cloak. As he walked along the street he saw a fine lady passing. With the lady were a number of servants, called attendants.

Can you guess who this fine lady was? She was the queen—Queen Elizabeth.

Just then the queen came to a muddy place in the road. She stopped a moment, not knowing what to do, for she had on a nice pair of shoes and she did not want to get them muddy.

What do you think the young man did? He took off his handsome velvet cloak and spread it over the muddy place in the road. Then the queen could walk across without soiling her shoes.

The queen was much pleased at what the young man did. His act showed that he was thoughtful and polite. Such gentlemen the queen liked to have about her, so she invited the young man to the palace. Soon he was one of the best known men in London.

This young man was Walter Raleigh. After some years the queen said that everybody should call him Sir Walter Raleigh. He became rich and was able to buy many fine cloaks. On his hat he often wore a black feather and a band of pearls. His shoes had sparkling jewels on them and were tied with white ribbons. Hanging to his belt was a shining sword.

Sir Walter Raleigh had a number of ships. Some of them he sent across the seas to this country. As you grow older and study more about the history of our country you will hear very often of Sir Walter Raleigh.

# FINDING A NEW WORLD

## (For October 12 - Columbus Day)

Did you ever find something nice when you were not looking for it?

Did you ever hunt for one thing and find something else that was better?

I am going to tell you a story about a man who once found something when he was hunting for something else.

This man was a brave sailor. He lived on the other side of the ocean, long ago. His name was Christopher—Christopher Columbus.

That is a long name, but I think you can remember it. Let us all say it loud, together—"Christopher Columbus!"

If I tell you what Christopher means you can remember it better. All names, you know, once meant something. Christopher means "Christ-bearer."

Columbus's father and mother were Christian people. They wanted their baby boy to grow up to be a good man, so they gave him a good name. Christopher is a good name.

When Christopher Columbus was a boy he used to watch the ships that came to his town. He lived in a town beside the sea. He wondered where the ships came from, and what they brought to his town. When they sailed out of the harbor he wondered what they were carrying away, and where they were going.

Often he talked with the sailors who lived on the ships. They told him many stories that pleased him. He said: "I'm going to be a sailor, too."

And he did become a sailor. Even before he was a man he was working on the ships and sailing here and there. Once the ship on which he was sailing took fire, and Columbus, with some other sailors, had to get down into the water. He swam and swam, till finally he got to the shore.

It is said that he swam six miles that time; but I think he must have had a plank or something of the kind that kept him from sinking.

Before Columbus was a man the Turks captured a big city in the East and would not let the Christians travel past that city any more. The Christians wanted to travel that way. They liked to go that way to India and China. India and China are two countries in the East where the Christians sold many things that they made to sell and bought many things that they needed. They still wanted to go to India and China.

Columbus said, "If we can't get to India and China by going east, let us get there by going west."

That sounded foolish, did it not? People who heard

Columbus say that thought it was foolish. They said:

"You can't get to India and China by going west!"

Columbus answered: "I think I can; for I believe that the earth is round like a ball. If it is, I can get there by going either way."

Then the people laughed more than ever. They thought that Columbus certainly was crazy. Hardly anybody in those days dreamed that the earth was round.

But Columbus believed it, and he said, "I'm going to prove it. I'm going to India by sailing west."

But it was easier said than done. Columbus was poor. He did not have money enough of his own to buy a ship, to hire sailors, or to get food for a long voyage.

For years and years he had to wait. Then the good queen of Spain helped him. She helped him fit out three little ships; she helped him get sailors and a supply of food.

Then Columbus was happy. He set sail and steered toward the west. He sailed and he sailed. His men said:

"It's no use—let's go back."

But Columbus said, "Sail on!"

They said, "We'll throw you out into the water and let you swim again if you don't take us back home!" Columbus said, "Sail on!"

At last, after they had sailed for eight or nine weeks,

*Columbus Sighting Land*

they came to a country and found some people there. Columbus said:

"This country must be India. The people look like the people of India."

So he called the people Indians, and they have been called Indians ever since.

But Columbus was mistaken. The country he found was this country of ours—this land in which we live: America, we call it.

So Columbus found something he was not looking for. He found a new world. He was looking for India but he found America.

It was in the month of October that Columbus found America. It was on the 12th day of the month. Today is the 12th of October—to-day is Columbus Day!

# THE MAYFLOWER AND THE PILGRIMS

## (For December 22 — Forefathers' Day)

The *Mayflower* was a little ship that came over the sea long ago. It carried a hundred people—men, women, and children.

These people were seeking a new home. They had left their old home across the sea because the king had said that they must not worship God in the way they thought was right. Because they had to travel so far to find a place to worship they were called Pilgrims.

It was winter when the Pilgrims came, and they had been on the ship three months or more. It took a long time to cross the sea in those days. They were anxious to get off the ship and to begin building houses to live in.

They looked at this place and that place along the shore, but no place seemed just right. When at last they did find a place to land and build their houses it was almost Christmas. It was only three or four days till Christmas Day.

First, some of the men got off the ship; then the women and children began to come ashore. They could not run the *Mayflower* quite up to the bank—the water was too shallow; so I suppose they all had to get into a small boat and step from that to the shore.

At the place where they landed from the small boat was a big rock, right at the edge of the water, and most of them—perhaps all of them—stepped on that rock when they jumped out of the boat.

They called the place Plymouth, after a city in England; and the big rock on which they landed they called Plymouth Rock.

That rock is still at Plymouth to-day, and it is still called Plymouth Rock. It is not at the edge of the water any more, for some of the shallow parts of the harbor have been filled up; but it is near the water, and it is marked so that visitors may easily find it.

If you go to Plymouth I am sure that you will want to see that rock. You will want to stand beside it and hear again the story of the Pilgrims, and how they left the *Mayflower* that winter day, so long ago.

After the Pilgrims left the *Mayflower* and began to build their houses on the shore many of them became sick. Before spring came nearly half of them died.

In April the *Mayflower* went back across the sea. The Pilgrims did not own the ship, they had only hired it to bring them over. Those who were still alive might have boarded the ship again and gone away, but they said that they would stay at Plymouth. It was their new home, and they believed that God would send them brighter days.

So they wrote letters to their friends across the sea, gave them to the sailors, and watched the *Mayflower* sail away. Then they went to work again, building log houses, clearing brush off the fields, and planting corn. Some friendly Indians showed them how to plant corn and catch fish. When autumn came they had plenty to eat, and in a few years Plymouth was a thrifty town.

Every winter now, a few days before Christmas, we think about the landing of the Pilgrims. The date on which they left the *Mayflower* and stepped on Plymouth Rock is called Forefathers' Day. It is a day when many good people in this country remember the faith their fathers had in God, and how brave they were to cross the sea in order that they might find a place to worship Him as they believed was right.

Here is a little rhyme about the Pilgrims. You may not understand all the words now, but sometime you will read it for yourself and understand it better. Listen!

*"Far o'er the Wintry Sea"*

Far o'er the wintry sea,
In faith that would be free,
The Pilgrims came
To death and fame,
Far o'er the wintry sea.

Upon a rocky shore,
To cross the seas no more,
    They built a home,
    Where waters foam,
Upon a rocky shore.

When winter days were long
They joined in prayer and song;
    They said, "The spring
    Good days will bring"—
When winter days were long.

Upon an April day
Their good ship sailed away;
    For weal or woe,
    They watched her go,
Upon an April day.

'Twas thus they built a home,
'Twas thus they ceased to roam;
    In days of yore,
    On Plymouth shore,
'Twas thus they built a home.

# AT THE FIRST THANKSGIVING

As you know, the first Thanksgiving in our country was held at the old town of Plymouth and lasted three days. It was in the month of November, in the year 1621.

The people who lived at Plymouth then were called Pilgrims. They had traveled around a great deal, and they had been sick and hungry for a long time; but in the spring they had planted corn and peas and barley. They had planted twenty acres of corn and six acres of peas and barley.

During the summer the barley grew fairly well and the corn grew very well; the peas failed. When autumn came they had no peas, but they had a good deal of barley and plenty of corn. They also had pumpkins. In the water were fish; in the forest were turkeys and deer.

The Pilgrims were not hungry any more, and they were very thankful; so they had a great thanksgiving feast.

Now, I am going to tell you about some of the persons who were present at that first Thanksgiving at Plymouth.

First, there was William Bradford. He was the governor of Plymouth, and he was the one who had told the people to have a thanksgiving.

Close to Governor Bradford was William Brewster. He is often called Elder Brewster, for he was the pastor at Plymouth. He preached to the people and prayed with them.

Elder Brewster loved books. When he died he had about three hundred books—a good many for that day.

Not far from Governor Bradford and Elder Brewster was Miles Standish. We call him Captain Standish, because he was a soldier and led the other soldiers of Plymouth when they had to fight.

Captain Standish was not a tall man, but he was very strong and active. He was also very brave. He had a long sword and a heavy gun. The gun was so heavy that he had to carry a prop to hold it up.

At the Thanksgiving feast some of the men and boys played ball and had games of running and jumping. All this was too tame for Captain Standish, so he and some of the other soldiers went out for a wolf hunt.

Another who was present at the first Thanksgiving was the good Indian chief, Massasoit. He was a friend to the Pilgrims, and he came to the feast with ninety of his braves. I doubt whether the food would have held out for so many if Massasoit and his men had not brought some with them. They brought five deer—and perhaps other things.

I suppose that two of the Indians that came with

Massasoit were Samoset and Squanto. Samoset had come to Plymouth in March and had cried out, "Welcome, Englishmen!" Squanto was also a good friend. He had taught the Pilgrims how to catch fish and plant corn.

Now if there had been nobody to cook the food and put it on the tables I imagine there would not have been so much eating; so we must not forget the ladies—the good women and girls. A Thanksgiving would not be very happy without them.

The women and the girls of Plymouth came around the long tables under the trees and put on the turkey, the venison, the fish, the bread, and the pumpkin pies. And I suppose they said, "Help yourselves!"

They wore plain dresses, long aprons, and pretty caps. One of the young women was named Priscilla— Priscilla Mullens. She was good at spinning with a wheel. She was also good at helping gentlemen to talk when they did not know exactly what to say.

Among the Pilgrim men were four hunters. Governor Bradford had sent them out some days before to shoot wild turkeys and other game for the feast. They soon came back with enough to last a week.

There was another man present at that first Thanksgiving whom you ought to remember. His name was John—John Alden. He was good at making tubs and buckets, and he could write well. He married Priscilla Mullens. Some day you will read about John Alden, Priscilla Mullens, and Captain Standish in a beautiful poem. John Alden lived for sixty-six years after that first Thanksgiving Day.

# FISHING WITH FIRE

Once a white boy went to live with the Indians. His name was Henry—Henry Spelman. He went to live with the Indians because he was hungry, and he knew that the Indians had plenty to eat. At Jamestown, where the white people lived, nearly everybody was hungry; but the Indians had corn and meat and fish.

Henry Spelman lived with the Indians a long time. He learned how to talk with them and he also learned how they did their work. He saw them plant corn, hunt ducks and deer, and make boats; and he saw them catch fish.

The Indians had many ways of catching fish. Sometimes they would take a big basket and hold it at a narrow place in the river where the fish had to pass. Sometimes they would build a dam across the stream and make big pockets in it. When the fish got into the pockets they could not find their way out. Sometimes they would make a spear by tying a sharp bone on the end of a long stick. An Indian would take this spear and watch the water till he saw a fish. Then he would jab the spear right into the fish and catch it fast.

But sometimes the Indians caught fish with fire.

Fishing with Fire

Wasn't that a strange way to catch fish? Henry Spelman often saw them do it. Shall I tell you how it was done?

It was done at night. The Indians would make a fire in a boat (a canoe, as they called it), and then push the boat out from the shore. Of course they would put a pile of earth into the boat first and build the fire on that, to keep the canoe from burning.

They used rich pine wood for the fire, because it burns fast and makes a good light. One man would stand by the fire to keep it burning brightly. At each end of the canoe would stand an Indian, with a long spear in his hand. They would push the boat along very gently, without splashing the water, without making any noise. They would not talk loud, either.

The light of the fire would shine down into the water, clear to the bottom of the river. The fish would be blinded by the light, and would lie still. Then the men with the long spears would jab them, one by one, and put them into the boat. This was the way the Indians fished with fire.

I imagine that Henry Spelman often went with the Indians on those fishing trips. At first he may have kept the fire burning; then perhaps he learned to stand up in one end of the boat and use the spear.

One had to be very quick and skillful at this work, or he would miss the fish and jab the spear into the ground or break it on a stone. If he were just a little awkward he might fall into the water.

# HORSESHOES OF GOLD

How many of you have seen a horseshoe? Have you ever found a horseshoe in the road? Who can draw a horseshoe on the blackboard?

Most horseshoes are made of iron, but I am going to tell you about some horseshoes that were made of gold.

A long time ago, before your grandfather or your grandmother was born, there was a good man in Virginia whose name was Spotswood—Alexander Spotswood. He was governor of Virginia. He lived down near the sea, where the country is level and sandy. All the people lived there at that time. Nobody had yet crossed the Blue Ridge Mountains.

Governor Spotswood decided to cross the Blue Ridge. He did not know just what was on the other side, and he wanted to find out. Nobody knew what was on the other side, and everybody wanted to know.

Some people thought that just west of the mountains would be found large bodies of water—great lakes; others thought that dreadful monsters, worse than bears and panthers, would be found there. Governor Spotswood decided to go and see for himself.

So he took a number of gentlemen with him and started. They packed up a great many things to eat and drink, for they knew that they would be away from home many days. They also took their guns to shoot deer and turkeys on the way and to defend themselves against hostile Indians. They had some friendly Indians as guides.

At first some of the party traveled in coaches, but when they got near the mountains they left the coaches and all rode on horseback.

On they went, through the woods and up the mountain slopes. At last, one day, they reached the top of the Blue Ridge and looked down on the other side. What did they see? They did not see any great lakes. They did not see any dreadful monsters worse than bears and panthers; but they did see a beautiful valley with a long river flowing through it.

On the sides of the valley were large forests, but along the river at many places were open meadows covered with tall grass. Here and there they may have seen a herd of deer or a group of buffaloes.

Governor Spotswood and his party went down to the river. Some went in swimming, others caught some fish. They had a good time for a day or two—then they started back home. When they got home they found that they had been gone nearly four weeks. After that the people of Virginia knew that the country west of the Blue Ridge was a good land in which to live.

But how about the golden horseshoes? I'll tell you.

Before Governor Spotswood and his party made this trip they did not have shoes on their horses. The horses did not need shoes in the level, sandy country near the sea. But when they went to the mountains they shod their horses with iron shoes. The mountains are steep and rocky.

The horseshoes of iron made Governor Spotswood think of horseshoes of gold. He did not want any of his friends to forget that trip over the mountains with him, so to help them remember it he gave each one of them a little horseshoe made of gold.

# RIDING A COLT

## (For February 22—Washington's Birthday)

Did any of you ever ride on horseback?

Horseback-riding is fine sport if you have a good horse and know how to ride.

Nowadays people do not ride horses as much as they did long ago. Now they ride mostly in carriages and automobiles; but when George Washington was a boy nearly everybody rode on horseback.

Did you know that to-day is George Washington's birthday? He was born on the twenty-second of February. To-day is the twenty-second; so I am going to tell you a little story about Washington.

Washington was a great man, and he was the first president of the United States. Everybody loves to honor him.

The story I am going to tell you is not about Washington as a man, but it is about Washington as a boy.

When Washington was twelve or fourteen years old his mother had a very wild young horse. What do we call a very young horse? A colt, yes. This was a colt.

Teaching colts to work and training them to be gentle is called breaking them. If colts are wild, this thing of breaking them is a dangerous business.

Well, it is said that George wanted to break that colt. It was very wild and fiery, but George wanted to get on its back.

George's mother was very strict. She said to him, "Do not try to ride that colt."

George was a fine fellow, and nearly always obeyed his mother; but one day he felt that he just had to break that colt.

By some means or other he got a bridle on the colt. I do not know whether he got a saddle on him or not. But all at once he jumped on the colt's back.

That was enough to frighten any horse. It scared that colt nearly to death, and he began to run and kick and try to get the boy off. But George stuck tight. He was a good rider, like Robert Lee and some other famous men I have read about.

In spite of all the running and jumping and kicking that colt could do, George held on.

All at once the colt gave a big jump. Then he fell down and lay on the ground. After a while he lay quite still. He was not "broken"—he was dead!

He had jumped and kicked so hard that he had burst a blood vessel somewhere in his body, and he had bled to death.

Now you may be sure that George Washington was very sorry for what he had done. He felt just as mean as he could feel, and he was ashamed to look his mother in the face. But he was no sneak. He walked home and told his mother what he had done.

She was very sorry that the colt was dead. She was still more sorry because George had not obeyed her; but she was glad that he did not tell a lie about it.

I am inclined to think that Washington was more careful after that to listen to what older persons said. He did not soon forget the day he had tried to break that colt.

# HATCHETS AND CHERRIES

(For February 22—Washington's Birthday)

Every winter, about the time of Washington's birthday, you see a great many little hatchets. You see them in shop windows for sale. You see people wearing them. You see pictures of hatchets on dinner cards and in newspapers. They are called Washington hatchets.

Along with these hatchets you often see cherries—nice red cherries! The hatchets and the cherries seem to go together.

I am going to tell you about these hatchets and cherries, and why you see them so much about the time of Washington's birthday.

Long, long ago somebody told a very pretty story about George Washington. The story was like this:

When George was a little boy his father gave him a little hatchet. Then, of course, George took his little hatchet and went around chopping into things—just to see how sharp the hatchet was.

In the garden was a nice young cherry tree. George's father prized that cherry tree very highly. But what did George do but go and hack into that nice cherry tree.

*George and His Father*

He hacked it and hacked it till the cherry tree was dead. He did it with his little hatchet.

Of course George's father was very sorry. George, too, was very sorry—after the mischief was done. But George didn't tell any stories about it. He just told his father the whole truth.

This pleased his father. Mind you, now, his father was not pleased because George hacked the cherry tree, but he was pleased because he told the straight truth about it.

Some people think that this story is not quite true; but we do know that Washington was a truthful boy and a truthful man; and it is because of this story about the hatchet and the cherry tree that we see so many cherries and little hatchets every year on Washington's birthday.

# GEORGE WASHINGTON AS A SCHOOLBOY

With the woods full of Indians and with all sorts of hard work to do, there was but little time to read books and go to school when George Washington was a boy. I doubt whether in all his life he ever saw a nice big schoolhouse for boys and girls. When he was a boy many of the girls never learned to read or write; and the boys often did not learn much more than reading, writing, and arithmetic.

George's father was a rich man, but George did not have a chance to go to school much of the time. And when he was eleven years old his father died. That is one reason, I suppose, why he did not go to school more. But he studied well while he was in school and learned more than some boys who went to school longer.

We know the names of two of his teachers. One was Mr. Hobby; the other was Mr. Williams. Mr. Hobby was his first teacher. He taught George to spell easy words and to make a start at writing. I imagine that George had a little slate and learned to write on that. Maybe he learned to write on a blackboard with a piece of white chalk, or maybe it was on a white board, with a piece of charcoal.

I suppose that Mr. Hobby wrote with a quill pen. Have you ever seen a quill pen? It is made of a big feather—often a turkey feather or a goose feather. In Washington's day people used quill pens instead of steel pens.

I do not know whether George learned to write with a quill pen while he was going to school to Mr. Hobby or not; but it was only a few years till he learned to write a good hand. He became a good penman, and usually took pains to write well. He tried to spell well too, but sometimes he got a word wrong.

While Washington was going to school to Mr. Williams he learned to do hard sums in arithmetic. He learned to measure land, to keep account of things he bought and sold, and to do many other things that were useful to him all his life.

About this time he read a little book that he always remembered. It was a book that told boys and young men how to behave themselves and how to live well. It contained many good rules for young people. George thought so much of some of those rules that he copied them down and read them over often. I am certain that those rules must have helped him to be a good boy and a good man. And when he grew up and became a great man his teachers must have been very proud of him.

You may be sure that Washington never forgot Mr. Hobby and Mr. Williams. But he had another teacher that we must not forget. Who do you think it was? It was his mother. From her he learned many of his best lessons.

# PLANTING THIRTEEN TREES

## (For Arbor Day)

Once a great man planted thirteen trees. I want you to remember his name if you can—his name was Hamilton. This is a rather long name. And his first name was still longer—Alexander.

There, now, you have it all: Alexander Hamilton! It is a long name, but it is easy to remember.

I am going to tell you about thirteen trees that Alexander Hamilton planted.

Alexander Hamilton was a great lawyer. He was also a brave soldier. He was a general in the Revolutionary War. After the war he had his home in New York City, where he had gone to school—to college—when he was a boy.

The old part of New York City is on an island about thirteen miles long. Mr. Hamilton's home was toward the upper end of this island. I imagine there must have been some farms there then, for he called his home "The Grange." This means "The Farm."

It was at the Grange that Hamilton planted the thirteen trees. He planted them in a circle, and they were all gum trees.

How many of you have seen a gum tree? A gum tree looks a little like a maple tree, a little like a poplar tree, and a little like an oak tree; yet it is different from them all. Its bark is rough, like the bark of a white oak, but it is darker in color. In the woods a gum tree grows rather tall and straight, like a poplar tree; and in the fall of the year its leaves turn to a beautiful red and gold, like maple leaves and oak leaves. But the gum leaves are more nearly round than oak or maple leaves.

Does anybody wonder why Mr. Hamilton planted just thirteen trees in that circle at the Grange?

I'll tell you why. Mr. Hamilton had helped General Washington, Mr. Madison, and others to build the United States. He was very proud of the great union of states, and he was hoping that it would grow larger and stronger.

Now in the Union at that time there were just thirteen states. In the flag there were just thirteen stars. That is the reason why Mr. Hamilton planted thirteen trees.

If you should ask me why he planted gum trees, I believe that I could guess the reason. Gum trees are very hard to split. Mr. Hamilton did not want anything to split the Union or any state in it.

The union of thirteen states grew, as Mr. Hamilton hoped it would. The thirteen trees also grew till they were tall. They reached out their branches and touched one another, just as good friends do when they form a circle.

That part of the city of New York where Mr. Hamilton planted the thirteen trees is now called Hamilton Place. But I am sorry to tell you that the trees are all gone. In the first place, they stood so close together that they choked one another. In the second place, visitors thought so much of Mr. Hamilton that each one wanted to cut off a little piece of one of the trees he had planted and carry it away as a relic. So you know what happened—the trees all died.

But the house in which Mr. Hamilton lived is still standing. From it one may see the Hudson River on the west and Long Island Sound on the east. Let us visit the Grange when we go to New York City.

# A HOUSE ON A MOUNTAIN

I'm going to tell you a story about a house on a mountain. It is a big house and a little mountain. The house is made of red bricks and the mountain is made of red dirt.

All around the little mountain, for miles and miles, a great deal of the earth is red. When white horses go along the roads in a dusty time they soon look red.

The mountain is called Monticello, which means "Little Mountain." It is near the city of Charlottesville, in the state of Virginia. The big house on top of the mountain is also called Monticello.

The house was built more than a hundred years ago by a famous man named Jefferson. His full name was Thomas Jefferson.

As a boy Thomas Jefferson played around the little mountain. When he became a man he built the house on top of the mountain.

First he leveled off the top of the mountain, so as to make a nice lawn of two or three acres. Then he built the house in the center of the level place.

The house has two fronts—one toward the north, the other toward the south. All around the house are beautiful trees, planted there many years ago. The sides of the mountain are still covered with forest, but here and there the trees have been cleared away to make a field or a garden.

A nice road leads up the mountain to the house. At the foot of the mountain, where the road starts up, is a big gate. The keeper of the gate lives beside it in a little red-brick cottage.

Near the cottage hangs a bell. When some one drives through the gate, going up the mountain, the gate-keeper rings the bell. This is to let the people in the big house know that some one is coming.

From the top of the little mountain one can look westward and see the town of Charlottesville, three miles away. When Mr. Jefferson was an old man he would often sit at Monticello and look toward Charlottesville. He would say to himself:

"What a fine place that is for a big school."

And he kept on working till a big school was started at Charlottesville. The school buildings were built of red bricks and of white marble brought from Italy. They stand on the hill just west of the town.

Mr. Jefferson loved that school. He called it the child of his old age. Hundreds of young men attend that school every year. It is called the University of Virginia, and it has grown very much since Mr. Jefferson's day.

Of course Mr. Jefferson is not living now. He died in the year 1826, and his grave was made on the little mountain, halfway up the road from the keeper's gate. The house on the top of the mountain has passed into other hands, but it is kept very much as the great man left it. Every year hundreds of visitors go there to see where Jefferson lived.

For eight years Mr. Jefferson was president of the United States. Long before that he wrote the Declaration of Independence. These are some of the things you will remember about him when you visit the house on top of the mountain.

# ROBERT LEE AND HIS MOTHER

## (For January 19—Lee's Birthday)

To-day I am going to tell you a story about a boy named Robert—Robert Lee. Robert Lee was born on the 19th of January, many, many years ago. This is the 19th of January, so this is his birthday. Let us find "19" on the calendar. Now we'll make a red mark around it, so we won't forget it.

Robert Lee's father died when Robert was eleven years old. He had two brothers and two sisters. Some of them were older than Robert was, but often they were away from home. Robert was always at home, so he looked after things around the house and the farm, and kept them in good shape. He carried a big bunch of keys. In the morning he would go around and unlock the doors; in the evening, about dark, he would go around again and lock them.

Do you wonder why Robert's mother did not carry the keys? I will tell you. His mother was sick nearly all the time. So Robert carried the keys and looked after his mother too.

For several years Mrs. Lee could not walk, but by the time Robert was seventeen he was strong enough to carry her about in his arms. She liked to go out driving; so Robert would hurry home from school in the evening and take her out for a drive.

The big old coach would come up in front of the door. Then Robert would take his mother up in his arms, carry her out, and tuck her in among the cushions. Then he would get in himself and they would take a long drive. Sometimes he would put old newspapers over the cracks in the curtains to keep out the cold. He did not mind the cold, but his mother did.

Maybe you wonder when Robert had time to play with the other boys. I do not know exactly—I don't believe that he spent very much time in playing.

Perhaps you think that he did not like to play, but he did. He was very fond of play, and he could play well. He was stronger than most boys of his age, and he could run and jump with any of them.

Let me tell you what a runner he was. Sometimes when the gentlemen would go fox-hunting, and ride on horseback, Robert would go along on foot. When a fox was started and the gentlemen would gallop away after him, Robert would begin to run.

He could not run as fast as the horses, but often he would keep on running for two or three hours without stopping. What do you think of that for running?

I imagine Robert Lee would have won in almost every game if he had gone to play with the other boys;

but he knew that his mother needed him at home. So he went home and looked after her.

Robert Lee was like George Washington—he loved his mother and tried to do all he could to make her happy.

# A BOY'S BOAT-RIDE

## (For February 12—Lincoln's Birthday)

Has any one had a birthday lately? Will any of you have a birthday soon?

To-day is somebody's birthday—can you guess whose it is?

Once there was a boy just as little as any of you, but when he was a man he was very tall—over six feet! He was not only a tall man—he was also a great man. He was president of the United States, and he did many things to make the people remember him.

His name was Abraham Lincoln. To-day is the 12th of February, and this is Abraham Lincoln's birthday. To help you remember this, I am going to tell you a story about Lincoln. I am going to tell you about a long boat-ride that he once took on a big, deep river.

When Lincoln took this long boat-ride his home was in Spencer County, Indiana. He was almost a man. He was tall and strong and could do a man's work. With him was another young fellow named Allen Gentry.

Allen's father had a lot of bacon and other produce that he wanted to sell; so Abe and Allen put it on a flatboat and took it down to New Orleans.

123

A flatboat is a large boat—long enough to reach across the road, and wide enough to hold a load of hay. It is not very deep and the sides are low; that is the reason it is called a flatboat.

Abe and Allen had a tent or some sort of roof over a part of their flatboat to keep off the rain and the hot sunshine. Abe stood at one end of the boat with a long oar; Allen stood at the other end—and they were off!

*Lincoln on the Flatboat*

First they went down the Ohio River about two hundred miles, till they came to the Mississippi River; then they went down the Mississippi till they came to the city of New Orleans.

Down the Mississippi was a long, long way. If the river were straight, it would be five hundred miles or more from the mouth of the Ohio to New Orleans. But the Mississippi is not straight—it is very crooked; so

I am pretty certain that Abe and Allen had to paddle down the "Father of Waters" about a thousand miles before they could sell their bacon. It was hard work, too, and you may be sure that Abe earned his eight dollars a month and board.

At night the flatboat was tied up to the bank of the river and the boys would sleep under their tent or roof. One night, while Abe and Allen were asleep, some robbers came on the boat. Allen got awake first. He listened a moment; then he cried out to Abe:

"Bring the guns, Lincoln, and shoot them!"

The boys had no guns, but Allen was trying to frighten the robbers. And Abe helped him. He grabbed up a big club and soon chased the robbers away.

When the boys got to New Orleans they could hardly sell the bacon for looking at the city. Abe had never seen a city like that before; so you cannot blame him for keeping his eyes and his ears wide open.

After the bacon and other things were sold Abe and Allen sold the flatboat, too. It was too far to take it back home. Besides, they had plenty of lumber at home to make another. When everything was sold they took another look at the city, then got on a steamboat that was going up the Mississippi and started for home. I suppose that the whole trip, down the river and back, lasted three or four months.

One day on this trip Lincoln made a dollar in about half an hour. Two gentlemen wanted to get on a steamboat that was going up the river. Lincoln got a little boat, took the gentlemen and their trunks in it, and rowed them out to the steamer. When they were safely on board each of them gave him fifty cents in silver.

He was very proud of that dollar. He had never earned one so quickly before. From that day on the world seemed wider and fairer to him, and he made up his mind that he could do great things.

Lincoln never forgot that boat-ride down the river, or what he saw in the city of New Orleans.

# A SWEET SONG

One reason we love birds is because they sing. And the world loves people who sing. If anybody gives us a good song, we always remember him for it.

We remember Francis Key because he gave us "The Star-Spangled Banner"; we remember Francis Smith because he gave us "America."

How many of you have heard a song that is called "Home, Sweet Home"?

A man by the name of Payne wrote that song. His full name was John Howard Payne. He died many years ago, but we love the song so well that we remember Mr. Payne and love him, too.

Payne was once a little boy in New York City. For a while he worked in a store, but he also went to school.

One day his father lost all his money and John had to stop going to school. This must have made him very sad, for he loved his books.

Presently he said, "I am going to do something to help my father make money." And he did. He began to play in a theater and made some money. This helped his father very much.

After Payne had played in New York some time, he went to Boston and Philadelphia and Baltimore. Then he went across the ocean to London and played there.

It was while he was in London that he wrote that sweet song, "Home, Sweet Home." Soon everybody in London was singing it. Then it was sung in other cities. Everybody liked it so well that in a little while people all over the world were singing "Home, Sweet Home."

Did Mr. Payne get rich? Did he receive a great deal of money for this song? He did not. He gave the world a sweet song, but he died poor.

I am not certain that Mr. Payne ever had a home of his own, but he taught other people to love their homes.

He was in a far-off land when he died. He was buried on a hill near the sea. Then, after many years, a good man had his body brought home to America, where the people like best to sing his song.

In the city of Washington is a beautiful white monument to Mr. Payne. Sometime when you go to Washington you may see it. At any rate, we shall always remember Mr. Payne when we sing "Home, Sweet Home."

## PART THREE

# THE GIRL WHO GATHERED BARLEY

Once in the long, long ago, a young woman left her own country and went to live in a strange land. She did this because she did not want to part from an older woman, who was her friend. The older woman's name was Naomi; the young woman's name was Ruth.

Ruth's old home was in the land of Moab. Naomi's old home was on the other side of the Jordan River, in Judea, near the town of Bethlehem. Naomi had lived in Ruth's country about ten years; then she returned to Bethlehem and Ruth went with her. Naomi, in returning to Bethlehem, was only going back home; but to Ruth the country around Bethlehem was new and strange.

If Ruth had not been a true-hearted girl, and if she had not loved Naomi, she would have stayed in the land of Moab.

When Ruth and Naomi came to Bethlehem it was the beginning of harvest. Barley was grown there more than wheat, and the barley harvest came in March or April. Ruth and Naomi arrived at Bethlehem just in time for the barley harvest.

Ruth and Naomi had no harvest of their own; they were poor; but as they watched the men and women going out to the barley fields with their sharp sickles, Naomi remembered her rich cousin Boaz. Boaz had large barley fields, and he had many reapers at work in his fields.

One morning Ruth said to Naomi, "Let me go to the barley fields. Perhaps some kind-hearted farmer will give me leave to pick up the heads of barley that the reapers drop."

Naomi consented and Ruth went to the fields.

Now it happened that Ruth got into a field that belonged to the rich man Boaz. It was early in the day and Boaz was still in the town, but his overseer told Ruth that she might follow the reapers and pick what barley she could find.

After a while Boaz came out into the field and saw Ruth. He said to the overseer, "What girl is this?"

The overseer answered, "It is the Moabite girl that came with Naomi when she returned home. She came to the field this morning and I gave her leave to glean among the reapers."

I suppose that Ruth heard what Boaz and the overseer said about her, and I imagine that she was somewhat frightened. She did not know what Boaz would say next. Perhaps she thought that he might order her to get out of his field.

Boaz came close to Ruth and spoke to her. This is what he said:

# The Girl who Gathered Barley

"Stay in my field all day—don't go to anybody else's field at all."

You may be sure that Ruth was glad that Boaz was so kind.

At dinner time Boaz gave Ruth part of his lunch. After dinner, when the reapers were taking their sickles to cut barley again, he said to them, softly, I think, so Ruth could not hear:

"Let fall some handfuls of barley on purpose for her."

So Ruth gleaned in the field of Boaz till evening. Then she beat out the heads she had gathered and found that she had nearly a bushel of barley.

When Naomi saw how much barley Ruth had gathered, and learned how kind Boaz had been to her, she was much pleased.

The next day Ruth gleaned in the fields of Boaz again. She continued her gleaning there till the barley harvest ended; and a month or two later, when the wheat harvest came, she was on hand again, gleaning in the fields of the rich man Boaz.

Doubtless you think that Boaz must have been pleased with Ruth, to show her so much kindness. He was pleased with her; and you need not be surprised when I tell you that Boaz after a while married Ruth.

Thus the girl who gathered barley became the wife of the rich man who owned the field. Her good habits and her faithfulness to Naomi proved to Boaz that she was a girl worth having.

If Ruth had not been so true to Naomi she might have lived and died in the land of Moab, and history would not even know her name. As it is, the world loves her. She became great and famous. Many of the persons named in the Bible were kin to her. For example, King David was her great-grandson.

When Ruth started to leave Moab and go to Bethlehem, Naomi was afraid she would get homesick, and advised her to remain in Moab; but Ruth held on to Naomi and went with her. And what she said to Naomi is worth remembering. These are her beautiful words:

> Entreat me not to leave thee,
> Or to return from following after thee:
> For whither thou goest, I will go;
> And where thou lodgest, I will lodge:
> Thy people shall be my people,
> And thy God my God:
> Where thou diest, will I die,
> And there will I be buried:
> The Lord do so to me, and more also,
> If aught but death part thee and me.

# THE KING'S CHRISTMAS

One Christmas long, long ago some men came to the city of Jerusalem. They were strangers there, for they had traveled hundreds of miles. They had come from the East, perhaps from the rich, flat country between the Euphrates and the Tigris River.

They came to Jerusalem with an eager question on their lips. They said:

"Where is He that is born King of the Jews? for we have seen His star in the East, and are come to worship Him."

They knew that a new king had been born, and they had come all the way from their own distant land to find him.

Jesus was the new king they were seeking, and he was then at Bethlehem only five or six miles from Jerusalem.

And there was a king at Jerusalem, too! His name was Herod. It is about King Herod's Christmas that I am going to tell you.

King Herod was very much disturbed when he heard the strangers asking for another king. He had been king for more than thirty years, and he did not want anybody to take his place. He still wanted to be king himself.

Now King Herod was very wicked. He decided to kill the new king. But he was also very sly and cunning. He said to himself:

"I am going to kill this new king, but I do not know yet where he is. I must find him before I tell anybody what I am going to do."

About that time some of the teachers in Jerusalem said that the new king would be found in Bethlehem.

Then Herod called the strangers into his private office. When he had locked the door he said to them:

"Go to Bethlehem and find the young king, and as soon as you find him come and tell me, for I am just as anxious as you are to find him and to worship him; but it will not do to let my people know it."

Herod was anxious to find Jesus, but he did not want to worship him.

Then the strangers went to Bethlehem and found Jesus. They worshiped him and presented unto him rich gifts. They were full of joy because they had found him.

But King Herod at Jerusalem was not full of joy. He was sad and troubled. It was not a happy Christmas for him.

He kept looking for the strangers to come back and tell him where Jesus was, but they did not come. Do you know why? God had warned them in a dream to steer clear of Herod; so they had gone home without coming near Jerusalem again.

Herod waited and waited. He wondered why the strangers did not come. At last he heard somebody say:

"Those men went home long ago—they did not come back to Jerusalem at all."

Then King Herod was very angry. He said:

"I'm not going to be fooled any longer! I'll kill that new king in spite of everything."

Then he called his soldiers. He said to them:

"Take your swords and go to Bethlehem. Kill every baby boy you can find there—and be sure you find them all!"

Was not that a cruel order for a king to give? But the soldiers obeyed him. They went to Bethlehem and killed all the little children they could find. Then they came away, but even after they left the town they could still hear the babies' mothers crying.

But still King Herod was not joyful. It was not a happy Christmas for him!

Do you think that anybody could have a joyful Christmas by making other people sad?

But I have not yet told you the best part of this story: King Herod's soldiers did not kill the little child Jesus. God warned his parents and they took him away before the soldiers reached Bethlehem.

# EASTER LILIES

Every year at Easter the flower windows are full of lilies. We like to have lilies in our homes and in our schoolrooms. On Sunday Easter lilies are carried to the churches. They seem to be quite at home amid the sound of prayers and sweet music.

For many years it has been a custom with Christian people to have lilies at Easter time. So Easter lilies have made for themselves a place in history.

Can you think of any reason why the lily has come to be the flower of Easter? I shall try to tell you why.

Easter is a great day of joy. In the long calendar of history there are many days of sorrow, many days of death, many days of darkness; but there are also many days of joy. Easter is a day of light, of life, of joy.

If you will remember that Easter is a great day of joy you will see, after awhile, why the lily is the Easter flower. I'll try to give you three reasons why it is so.

The first reason grows out of an old story of a beautiful, good woman. This woman, so the story goes, grew the first lily—a white lily. Because she was thought to be such a good woman the lily was thought to be a good flower.

This old story about the origin of the lily made people look upon it as a flower that is suitable for use in churches. They said, "It was given by a good woman; it is intended for good uses."

The lily is the flower of Goodness.

The second reason grows out of the white color of the lily. Not all lilies are white, but many of them are white; and white is the color we think of as belonging to lilies.

White is the color of perfect light. It is the color of snow. It is the color that stands for virtue and purity. The right kind of conduct we call white conduct. White robes and white snow and white living give forth white light. White lilies love light and give light. They smile forth most sweetly in the beautiful white light of dawn.

The lily is the flower of Light.

The third reason why lilies are used so much at Easter is because of what Christ said about them. Whenever we think of the lilies we have to think of his beautiful words about the lilies.

It may be that the lilies of the Holy Land were not all white, but the Master loved them, of whatever color they were; and he pointed to them when he wanted to teach the people faith.

He thought that people ought not to fret and worry so much, but ought to trust God more. He thought that we ought to learn a lesson of faith from the lilies, and keep on growing stronger and more perfect every day. So he pointed to the lilies and said:

"Consider the lilies of the field, how they grow; they toil not, neither do they spin: and yet I say unto you that even Solomon in all his glory was not arrayed like one of these. Wherefore, if God so clothe the grass of the field, which to-day is, and to-morrow is cast into the oven, shall he not much more care for you, O ye of little faith?"

The lily is the flower of Faith.

The Master wanted his disciples to have faith in order to be ready for the first Easter morning. He went away and left them in darkness, but he said that he would come back and bring the light. He wanted them to believe him—he wanted them to have faith and to look forward. That first Easter morning was a morning of joy, but it took faith to wait for it and to be ready for it.

The Master still wants his people to have faith. It is the faith of the Christian that makes him ready for Easter, and makes Easter to him a morning of joy.

Do you not see now why we love white lilies at Easter? The white lily is the flower of Goodness, the flower of Light, the flower of Faith. Goodness and Light and Faith make Easter Joy. Easter is a great day of joy. Easter lilies are flowers of joy.

# SAINT VALENTINE

## (For February 14)

The 14th of this month (February) is called St. Valentine's Day. You have often heard of this day and of St. Valentine, and now I am going to tell you who St. Valentine was and what St. Valentine's Day means.

St. Valentine was a good man who lived in Europe nearly two thousand years ago. He was a teacher—a Christian teacher. At that time the emperor at Rome was not a Christian. The emperor hated the Christians and had many of them put to death.

Those Christians who were put to death because of their faith in Christ are called martyrs. St. Valentine was a martyr; for it is said that the emperor had him put to death because he kept on teaching men to be Christians.

It was many, many years after the death of St. Valentine before people began to call any day after him; but at last the 14th of February was chosen, and it has been called St. Valentine's Day ever since. In France, in England, and in the United States the day has been celebrated every year for a long time.

In France and in England ladies and gentlemen on

St. Valentine's Day used to play a game like this: The names of all the ladies were written on pieces of paper and thrown into a box. Then the gentlemen came up, one at a time, and were blindfolded. When one was blindfolded he put his hand into the box and drew out a piece of paper. The lady whose name was on the paper he drew could then claim him as her "Valentine" for a whole year.

*"Sometimes the gentleman would make the lady a present"*

Sometimes they would exchange presents; sometimes the gentleman would make the lady a present, but receive none from her.

In our country St. Valentine's Day is celebrated by the exchange of letters, post cards, pictures, or other gifts. The pictures that we call valentines are of many different shapes, sizes, colors, and styles. Some of them are very pretty, some are very ugly.

Years ago in this country gentlemen used to cut out beautiful heart-shaped valentines with their penknives and send them to their lady friends. We do not see many valentines of this sort nowadays, but perhaps your grandmothers may have some hid away among their old letters and books.

It seems to me that the sending of ugly valentines is not a nice custom. St. Valentine was a good man, his very name means goodness and strength; and St. Valentine's Day ought to be a good day.

It is a day when good friends try to make one another happy. It is a day not for ugly things, but for beautiful things—for beautiful words, beautiful pictures, beautiful thoughts, beautiful deeds.

> Now let us have a play,
> In good old-fashioned way:
> He's with us yet,
> And we have met
> Saint Valentine to-day!
>
> If you a friend will be—
> A Valentine to me—
> I'll promise true,
> The whole year through,
> A Valentine to thee!

# BALBOA'S DISCOVERY

## (For September 26—Pacific Day)

One day in September, four hundred years ago, a young man climbed to the top of a mountain. The Indians had told him that he could see from the mountain-top a great water.

And he was not disappointed. As he stood on the height and looked southward he saw a great ocean stretching away and away, far beyond the reach of his keen eyes. He called it the South Sea, because he saw it as he looked toward the south.

That young man was Vasco Balboa, a Spaniard. He had come to the New World soon after it had been discovered by Columbus. He had gone from place to place, seeking gold, seeking knowledge; and he found knowledge on that mountain-top. He discovered the South Sea—the Pacific Ocean, we call it. Balboa was the first man from Europe to see that part of the Pacific.

Balboa was a handsome young fellow—tall, bright-eyed, and active. He was brave and had good manners. He also had the gift of making friends, but his skill and daring, his energy and his success, also made him enemies.

His enemies brought about his death while he was still young and handsome. He was accused of being a traitor, and of having done things that he was not told to do.

"I am no traitor," he declared; "and if I have done things I was not told to do I did them for the good of Spain."

But his enemies were jealous of him and they prevailed. Balboa was put to death.

But nothing can rob him of the honor due him. He made a great discovery, and History will always write his name in large letters; then Geography will come and place a wreath upon it; for Balboa helped Geography as well as History.

Now, let me tell you a few more things about Balboa's discovery. The mountain from which he first saw the Pacific Ocean was on the Isthmus of Panama, close to the place where the great Panama Canal now goes through; and the Canal was opened just four hundred years after Balboa was there.

The men who dug the Canal thought of Balboa often while they were at work; for one of the towns near the Canal is called Balboa Heights.

When the Canal was finished a big fair was held at San Francisco, and nearly everybody who went to that fair heard of Balboa. Indeed, many thousands of persons who did not go to the fair also heard of him; for his picture was printed on papers that told about the fair, and these papers were sent all over the world.

It is hard to rob a man who does a great deed.

In ending this story I must see how well you remember the first part of it.

In what month did Balboa discover the Pacific? Yes, in September. Now, do you know on what day of September it was?

It was on the 26th.

Thus you see why I have told you this story to-day. To-day is the 26th—the anniversary of Balboa's great discovery. We may call this day Pacific Day or Balboa Day.

# THE MAN WHO
# WAS THIRSTY

Many, many years ago, soon after the white men first came to America, a brave captain from Spain was sailing along the coast of Florida. We call it Florida now because he called it Florida then—"the land of flowers."

This captain's name was John Ponce. At any rate, that was part of his name. He had a long name, the rest of which you will learn some day.

John Ponce was in a ship with some other men. They had come to explore the country, and they thought Florida was an island. One day they became very thirsty. You know that people in a ship may die of thirst, for usually the water all around them is so salty that they cannot drink it.

Most of the Indians that John Ponce met in Florida tried to kill him, but a few were friendly, and it happened on the day when he and his men were so thirsty that he met a friendly Indian. This Indian perhaps came along in a canoe.

John Ponce said to the friendly Indian, "My men and I are very thirsty—where can we find water to drink?"

Said the Indian, "If you will come with me I will take you to a fountain where, if an old man like you drinks, he will get young again."

This was perhaps the Indian's way of saying that the water was very good.

John Ponce went with the Indian to the shore and there, sure enough, he found a spring of good sweet water.

Near the fountain was a temple in which the Indians worshiped. Ponce was so grateful to them that he gave them a sundial for the temple. By means of it they could tell the time of day.

Near the fountain and the temple Ponce and his men buried a silver helmet and a stone cross. These things were found there just a few years ago by some men who were digging in the ground.

Many persons have thought that John Ponce went to Florida in order to hunt for a fountain that would make him young again, but this is probably not true. The chances are he went to get acquainted with the country and sought the beautiful spring with the Indian as a guide, as I have told you, because he was very thirsty.

Many years later John Ponce went back to Florida and was killed by the Indians.

# JAMESTOWN DAY

## (For May 13)

How would you like to be out on the ocean all winter, in a ship? I know of some men who had that experience. They got aboard some little ships in the month of December, just a few days before Christmas, and they did not leave the ships till the next May.

But those men made some interesting history, so I must tell you about them.

Those men—there were about a hundred of them were Englishmen, for the most part. One of them was Captain John Smith. You have heard of him, have you not? Captain John Smith and his companions boarded those little ships in England and came across the sea to Virginia. When they reached Virginia they began to build a town. They called the town Jamestown, after the king of England; and Jamestown was the first English town in this country.

They began work at Jamestown on the 13th of May, in the year 1607. That was more than three hundred years ago, but we must not forget the day. It seems to me that we ought to call May 13 "Jamestown Day," just as we call December 22 "Forefathers' Day" or "Plymouth Rock Day."

Captain John Smith and his companions built their little town on an island in the James River, about forty miles up the river from its mouth. The place was not an island then, but it was almost an island. It is an island now. It is a rather large island for a river island. It contains more than a thousand acres.

In the month of May the new country was very beautiful. The oak trees were full of light-green leaves. The pine trees were armed with dark-green needles, and on the ground under them was a nice brown carpet. At many places were dogwood bushes full of snow-white blossoms, and here and there among them were little trees with blossoms of red. The air was sweet with the breath of flowers, and the tired men on the ships were happy to reach such a pleasant land.

Captain Smith thought that heaven and earth had never made a nicer place for man to live.

But he was to learn that sorrow could come to Jamestown, too. Food soon became scarce, men fell sick, and many graves were dug before Jamestown could claim a place in history.

John Smith was not the leader at Jamestown at first; but when hard times began to come he seemed the only man who could do things and tell the others what to do. So he took affairs in hand. If it had not been for him, the settlement at Jamestown would probably have been a failure, as many others of that time were.

The first houses at Jamestown were very poor structures. They were made of logs, rails, poles, brush, and dirt. A few of them were only old tents.

Reverend Robert Hunt was the pastor at Jamestown, and one of the first buildings was a sort of church. If I tell you what Captain Smith said about that church you will get a good notion of what the other houses were like. In his book he says:

"We did hang an awning (which is an old sail) to three or four trees, to shadow us from the sun; our walls were rails of wood; our seats unhewed trees, till we cut planks; our pulpit a bar of wood nailed to two neighboring trees. In foul weather we shifted into an old rotten tent, for we had few better. This was our church till we built a homely thing like a barn, set upon crotchets, covered with rafts, sedge, and earth, as were also the walls."

Then he goes on to say that the best houses were worse than the church, and that they did not altogether keep out either wind or rain.

Near Jamestown, a few years ago (1907), thousands of people came together to hold a great celebration. It was called the Jamestown Exposition, and it lasted for several months. It celebrated the founding of Jamestown, three hundred years before. In three hundred years our country has grown strong and great.

Only a few people live at Jamestown now, but they are always ready to show visitors where Captain Smith and his companions made their settlement. The place is marked by a splendid monument to Captain Smith and by the tower of an old brick church.

Let us mark May 13 as another red-letter day in our history calendar. It is Jamestown Day.

# WASHINGTON AS A SURVEYOR

At Greenway Court, in the Valley of Virginia, not many miles from the Shenandoah River, stands a little stone house. It is called "The Office." It is very old, for it was built when George Washington was a young man. Washington was often in that little stone house, for his good friend, Sir Thomas Fairfax, lived at Greenway Court.

When Washington was sixteen years old Sir Thomas was nearly sixty, but they were good friends for all that. Sir Thomas had miles and miles of land out in the valley and in the mountains, and he hired his young friend George to go out and explore it and measure it for him. Washington had a little book in which he wrote down what he saw, what he did, and what he found out about the land. When he came back to Greenway Court he and Sir Thomas would sit down in the little stone office and talk it all over. When people came to buy land of Sir Thomas he would take them into the office and tell them what Washington had said about the land.

How would you like to go out and live in the woods? That is what Washington did when he was sixteen and seventeen years old. And it took him two or three years to survey all of Sir Thomas's land. After a month or two in the forests he would go back to Greenway Court and have a talk with Sir Thomas. Then he would take his gun and his compass and his chain, get on his horse, and go back to the woods and the mountains again. Sometimes he would ride his horse through rivers and creeks. Sometimes he would ride through large open plains covered with grass, and there he might see herds of big black buffaloes. Deer were often seen. Wild turkeys were plentiful; and once in a while he would see a bear.

Part of the time another young man was with him. His name was Fairfax. He was a nephew of Sir Thomas. And I suppose that they had a few servants most of the time to help with the surveying.

Washington and his companions were often wet and cold. If they wanted meat for dinner or supper they had to shoot a turkey or a deer. They cooked the meat by holding it on sticks over the fire. They did not have dishes to wash, for instead of plates they used large chips. When they wanted a drink of water they perhaps lay down on a flat rock and drank out of a running stream.

Sometimes they found a hunter's camp and spent the night with him. Sometimes they came upon the rude log cabin of a settler and lodged there. But even then they did not often have a bed to sleep in. They would lie down on the floor, before the open fire, and sleep the best they could.

Now and then they met a party of Indians, but the Indians were usually friendly. One night they stayed in an Indian camp and saw the Indians have a war-dance. In their paint and feathers, waving their tomahawks, they danced and howled round and round about the big camp fire, while the young surveyors looked on in wonder.

Those two or three years in the woods, surveying for Lord Fairfax, were worth a great deal to Washington. In the first place Sir Thomas paid him well—about $20 a day; besides, he learned many things that were useful to him later. Years afterwards, when he had to fight the Indians and lead soldiers through the forests, he knew where he was and what he was about.

At Greenway Court he also had a chance to read some books that Sir Thomas had. Thus he learned many things. In the little stone office was a corner for his gun, I imagine; another for his compass and chain; and there were also a peg for his hat and a table for his pen and his book.

# A CITY ON A ROCK

In the year 1608, the next year after the English settled at Jamestown, a brave Frenchman began to build a town in Canada.

The Frenchman's name was Samuel Champlain. He did so much for the French people in Canada that he is often called the Father of Canada.

The town that Champlain began to build in 1608 he named Quebec. He got the name from the Indians. His town is now a city—the oldest city of Canada and it is still called Quebec.

The older part of Quebec is perched high upon a great rock. At the foot of the rock flows a broad, deep river, the St. Lawrence. From the level of the river straight up to the top of the rock it is more than three hundred feet. It was on top of this great high rock that Champlain built his town. From it one may look down and see the big river for many miles.

When one is on top of the rock at Quebec he finds that there are some large fields just behind the city. These fields are called the Plains of Abraham.

Now, I don't believe that you could ever guess just how those fields got that name, so I'll tell you. Long ago they were owned by a man named Abraham. This man was a pilot on the St. Lawrence River. Ever since that time they have been called the Plains of Abraham.

Three famous generals have been killed at Quebec: General James Wolfe, General Louis Montcalm, and General Richard Montgomery. Wolfe was an Englishman, Montcalm was a Frenchman. Wolfe and Montcalm were both killed on the same day, in the year 1759. Montgomery was an American. He was killed in the year 1775, soon after the beginning of the Revolutionary War. At that time the Americans were trying to take Quebec from the British.

Now I must tell you a little more about Wolfe and Montcalm; for every boy and girl who studies history ought to link the names of Wolfe and Montcalm with those of Champlain and Quebec.

In 1759, about the middle of the French and Indian War, the British were trying to take Quebec from the French. The French soldiers in Quebec were commanded by General Montcalm. Montcalm at this time was forty-seven years old and had often proved that he was skillful and brave.

The British soldiers, who were trying to capture Quebec, were commanded by General Wolfe. Wolfe was only thirty-two, but he was just as skillful and just as brave as Montcalm.

Because Quebec is up so high on the steep, rugged cliffs, General Montcalm and his men felt pretty safe. They thought that General Wolfe and his men could never force their way up to the top of the great rock. If they did succeed in doing that, they would still have to break through the city's strong walls.

But Wolfe and his men found a way. One night, when all was still, they got into their boats and landed on the bank of the river just at the foot of the high cliffs. Somebody found a steep, narrow path up the side of the rock, and by the next morning, when Montcalm looked out, Wolfe and his army stood on the Plains of Abraham, close to the city.

Montcalm said to his soldiers: "We'll go out and fight them."

"So we will," his soldiers replied; and so they did.

The Plains of Abraham were red that day, not only with British coats, but also with the blood of many brave men—French and British.

At last the French were beaten and the British took Quebec; but in the hour of victory—in the hour of defeat—both Wolfe and Montcalm fell to rise no more.

Wolfe said he died happy because of his victory; Montcalm said he was glad to die because he would not then see the surrender of Quebec.

Ever since that bloody day in 1759 the British flag has waved above Quebec—the city on the rock; and near the flag is a tall monument to Wolfe and Montcalm.

# WHEN NEW YORK CITY HAD A WALL

Long ago it was, when New York City had a wall. The place was not called New York then, and it was not a city either. It was just a little town, of Dutch people mainly, down on the point of an island, right at the gate of the sea.

The town at that time was called New Amsterdam; for some of the Dutch settlers had come from old Amsterdam, across the seas.

On three sides of New Amsterdam no wall was needed, for the deep water was on three sides; but on the fourth side a wall was built.

The wall at first was made of logs and dirt. The logs stood up on end, close together, and the earth was banked up against them. The wall reached clear across the island, from East River to North River. North River is also called Hudson River. The island (Manhattan Island) is narrow down near the point, so the wall was only about half a mile long.

Within that small space, about half a mile square, New Amsterdam stood. On the east, on the west, on the south was the water; on the north was the wall. The sturdy Dutchmen felt secure. The wall, they thought, would keep the Indians out, and they were not much afraid of anybody coming on the water to attack them.

But the attack, when it came, did come from the side of the water. A dozen years after the wall had been built some English soldiers came in ships, with cannon, and captured New Amsterdam. They changed the name to New York, but they allowed the Dutch people to remain.

The English rebuilt the wall and made it stronger. Some parts of it they built of stone. For many years afterward the town was all inside the wall.

Then the little wall could hold New York no longer. Houses were built outside the wall, farther and farther up the island. Since the day New York City jumped over the wall nobody has ever tried again to wall it in. To do so now would take a wall sixty miles long.

*"When New York City Had a Wall"*

Many cities in the Old World had walls; in the New World very few have had them. The wall that New York once had has all been torn away. It was not left even as a relic for the boys and girls who study history. But we can tell where the old wall stood. It ran across the island right where Wall Street is now.

# WHEN CHICAGO
# WAS A VILLAGE

Every great city was once a small town—only a village at first. The wonderful thing is how rapidly some villages have grown up into great cities. In the United States are many instances of such wonderful growth. For example, less than ninety years ago Chicago had less than a hundred people. There are some men and women living to-day who may remember when Chicago was only a village.

The name of Chicago, like the name of Quebec, was borrowed from the Indians. It was perhaps derived from an Indian word meaning "wild onion"—a plant which grew abundantly about the place.

Chicago was a famous meeting place for the Indians long before the white men came. The first white men to visit the place were Frenchmen from Canada.

The first permanent settler was a mulatto from the island of Haiti. His name was John Baptist, and he built his cabin about the year 1779.

The first white settler of American birth was John Kinzie. Mr. Kinzie was born at Quebec. He lived in New York City for a while; then he went west and located at

Chicago in 1804. The same year a fort was built near by and named Fort Dearborn.

In 1812 nearly all the white people at Chicago, excepting Mr. Kinzie and his sons, were killed by the Indians. The next day the Indians burned the fort; but this was rebuilt in 1816. A part of this old fort stood till the year 1856.

The first regular school in Chicago was opened in 1816—the same year in which Fort Dearborn was rebuilt. The first sermon in English was preached in 1825. French missionaries had no doubt preached there in French many years before.

The first post office was opened in 1831, and the people of Chicago began to get their mail more regularly. The next year the first frame business houses were erected. Nearly all the buildings up to that time had been made of logs. And in 1834 something came that made a great deal of noise. It churned the water, it burned up a lot of wood, it blew great clouds of smoke into the air. It was the first steamboat that came to Chicago.

Chicago is built on the shore of a great lake—Lake Michigan. This makes it possible for boats of all kinds to come and go easily.

At the spot where the city started, a little river pushes its way out into the lake. This is called the Chicago River. Fort Dearborn stood near the mouth of the little river, and the village clustered around the fort. There John Baptist, John Kinzie, and others lived. There Ellen Kinzie, the first white child, was born.

One of the streets in the old part of Chicago is called Dearborn Street to-day; and another that crosses it is called Kinzie Street. Some of the other streets have French names, some have Indian names. All of these names remind us of the days when Chicago was a village.

# HOW THANKSGIVING GREW

The first governor who said, "Let us have a thanksgiving," was William Bradford, at Plymouth; the first President who proclaimed a thanksgiving day was George Washington, at New York.

The custom of having a big Thanksgiving Day all over the country every year grew up gradually from having little thanksgiving days here and there, once in a while. I am going to show you, if I can, how Thanksgiving Day grew.

As I said, the first governor to proclaim a thanksgiving was Governor Bradford, at Plymouth. The first thanksgiving at Plymouth was held in November, 1621. That was the first in this country. In 1623 there was another thanksgiving at Plymouth because a good rain came when it was much needed.

At Salem, another town north of Plymouth, the people had a public thanksgiving in the summer of 1630 because some ships came and brought them food.

At Boston, in 1631, there was a thanksgiving in the month of February. A ship had come to Boston, bringing food and other supplies.

Plymouth, Salem, and Boston are all in Massachusetts. Massachusetts and five other states (Maine, New Hampshire, Vermont, Rhode Island, and Connecticut) make up what we call New England. In many towns of New England it soon became the custom to have a public thanksgiving every year.

During the Revolutionary War (1775-1783) Congress every year asked the people to observe a day of prayer and thanksgiving. Then, soon after the Revolution ended, General Washington was the first President, and the first one to proclaim a thanksgiving day, as I have said. That was in 1789.

President Washington named Thursday, the 26th of November (1789), as a day of national thanksgiving. He urged the people to thank God for his blessings, to ask him to pardon their sins, to pray to him for strength to do all their duties, private and public, and to ask him to make our national government a blessing to all.

I suppose that Thanksgiving was still observed in the towns of New England every year, but the Presidents for a long time did not issue a Thanksgiving proclamation every year. At some places, then, a thanksgiving day was kept, whether the President said so or not; and at other places there was no thanksgiving, even when the President requested it.

Since the year 1863 the Presidents have appointed a thanksgiving day every year. For some time after that date the day was not observed everywhere, but for a number of years past it has been kept all over the United States.

Now, therefore, we have a real national Thanksgiving. The day is appointed by the President, and his proclamation is sent all over the country. At the same time, or soon afterward, the governor of each state also issues a Thanksgiving proclamation, appointing the same day that the President names.

In every part of our great country the people have come to look forward to Thanksgiving, from year to year, as a day that we cannot give up. It has grown from small beginnings in little towns to a great day for all the land. At first Thanksgiving Day was a New England holiday; now it is a national holiday.

# WHITE FRIENDS AND RED FRIENDS

On the bank of a great river one day, more than two hundred years ago, some men gathered wood and built a camp fire. The camp was pitched under a large elm tree. Some of the men who gathered around the camp fire were white men, but most of them were red men. With the red men were their wives and children.

One young white man did most of the talking. He said that he had come over the ocean to be a friend to the red men, and that he wanted to buy some land of them in order that he might live near them.

The red men sat still and listened while the young white man talked. They looked at his plain clothes and at his broad-brimmed hat. They wondered what sort of man he was. But when they looked into his kind, honest face they felt sure that he was a good man, and they began to trust him. They felt as if they would like to be his friends and to have him for a neighbor.

After some of the red men had spoken the young white man talked again. By this time he knew that the red men would be his friends, and that they would sell him all the land he wanted; so he began to pay them for the land.

He gave them rolls of cloth, such as they had never seen before. He gave them axes, knives, beads, and red paint. He knew that the Indians liked red paint. He also gave them shirts, shoes, and some guns. The old Indians kept pretty quiet, but the youngsters could not help showing how glad they were to get all those nice things.

*Penn Paying for His Land*

Then the red men gave the white man a fine belt of wampum. Wampum was something that the Indians made by weaving strings of shells or beads together. They prized wampum very highly. It was money to them.

When they gave the young man the wampum belt they said:

"We will be your friends as long as the sun shines."

Then they lighted a big pipe, called the pipe of peace. This they passed around from one to another in order that all might take a whiff. It was understood that all who smoked the big peace-pipe would be friends.

After a while the sun went down and the stars came out. Then, it may be, the moon came up and smiled across the river at the group under the tree. If so, the red men doubtless pointed to the moon and said:

"As long as the moon shines we will be your friends."

The promises of the white men and the red men, made under that big elm tree, were faithfully kept. A city was built there called the "City of Brotherly Love," and William Penn and the Indians were always friends.

William Penn was the young white man who made the treaty with the Indians. He also laid out the city of Philadelphia—the City of Brotherly Love. The great state of Pennsylvania is named after him and his father.

If you should go to Philadelphia and walk along the bank of the Delaware River, you would find a tall, white stone. That stone marks the place where William Penn met the Indians under the big elm tree. The tree blew down a hundred years ago, but we must not forget where it stood.

# A FAMOUS TREE

## (For Arbor Day)

The biggest and the oldest thing alive is a tree. It stands in Sequoia National Park, California. It is 280 feet high, and its diameter is thirty-six and a half feet. It is three or four thousand years old. When Moses was born it was perhaps just beginning to grow, but it has been growing ever since. It is called the General Sherman Tree.

Other big trees near the General Sherman bear the names of Grant, Lincoln, and Washington.

All these trees are famous for their size and their age. In other parts of the world are trees that are famous in history. For example, in Boston, Massachusetts, is the Washington Elm. Under that elm General George Washington took command of the American army at the beginning of the Revolutionary War, in the year 1775. Another famous elm tree stood for many years in the city of Philadelphia. Under it William Penn made his treaty of friendship with the Indians.

But the tree about which I am going to tell you most to-day stood long ago in the city of Hartford, Connecticut. It is known in the history of our country as the Charter Oak.

This oak was about six feet in diameter, and there was a large hole in it about two feet above the ground. This hole was large enough to admit a small child.

Now, I'll tell you why this oak was called the Charter Oak.

In the early days of our history the people of Hartford had a charter that they prized very highly. A charter is a law by which people govern themselves. But on one occasion the king sent to Hartford a man who said that he was going to take away the charter.

A meeting was held in the town hall. It lasted a long time—till after dark, and candles were lighted. When the meeting had continued awhile longer, and it looked as if the king's man was determined to have the charter, all at once the lights went out and the room became pitch dark.

When the candles were relighted the charter was gone. But the king's man did not have it, and he did not get it; for he did not know where it was.

Only a few men knew where it was. They had hidden it in the hole in the big old oak. There the charter remained for about two years, and the people of Hartford did not have to surrender it. Ever since that time the old oak tree has been known as the Charter Oak.

The Charter Oak stood in Hartford till the year 1856. In August of that year a hard storm blew it down. At that time some persons examined it very carefully and came to the conclusion that its age was nearly one thousand years.

In the city of Hartford to-day a white marble slab marks the spot where the famous Charter Oak stood; and the street that passes in front of the place is called Charter Oak Avenue.

# THE TEA PARTY AT BOSTON

One winter day in the year 1773 a big crowd of men in Boston met together and arranged for a tea party. Usually a tea party is managed by the ladies, but this one was taken in hand by the men.

It was nearly Christmas, and perhaps the day was cold, but the house was crowded. This proved that the men were in earnest. In fact, they were angry. They were hungry for tea, but they were angry because the king of England had sent them some and wanted them to drink it.

This, I know, sounds queer; so I must try to explain to you just how it was.

At that time all the people of this country were subjects of the king; but the king and his officers had been doing some things that our people did not like. For example, they had been trying to make our people pay taxes in a way that our people thought was wrong.

Finally the king and his officers decided to try another plan. They said:

"We'll take the tax off some things but we'll put it on something else—we'll put it on tea. They'll pay the tax on tea—they like tea."

But the king and his officers were mistaken. The Americans did like tea, but they were tired of paying tax to the king, on tea or on anything else. So they said:

"We'll not buy the king's tea."

But the king or some of his men sent three ships to Boston—three ships loaded with tea. They seemed determined to make the people take tea. The people were just as much determined that they would not take tea—at least, not in the way the king wanted them to take it.

So the men of Boston held a meeting, as I have said. Thousands of people attended the meeting.

"We're hungry for tea," they said, "but we don't want tea with the king's tax on it. We won't have tea with his tax on it."

But in the harbor were three ships loaded with tea. The king had sent them there; and the king's officers at Boston said that they must be unloaded there.

Finally somebody in the crowd asked a question —not very loud:

"Will tea mix with salt water?"

Then somebody else whispered: "Why not have Boston harbor for a teapot to-night?"

"Sure enough," said another; "if the king is so anxious for us to use his tea, let's use it in a way he'll remember."

And so the talk went on—not out loud, but loud enough for everybody except the king's officers to hear.

"We'll unload the king's tea."

"We'll use up all of it, but we won't drink any of it."

So the men of Boston arranged to have a big tea party that very night.

About the time the clock struck nine that night somebody began to shout, "Indians! Indians!"

Then a loud, fierce war-whoop rang through the quiet streets.

But somehow everybody seemed expecting it—everybody except the king's officers.

Then a troop of about fifty Indians came marching down the street.

"Mohawks!" was the cry.

They did look like Mohawk Indians, but nobody seemed to be afraid of them—nobody except the king's men and the sailors on the tea ships.

Straight to the harbor the red men marched. On board the tea ships they rushed. With their tomahawks they knocked open the chests of tea—350 of them—and out into the salt water of Boston harbor the tea went!

Boston harbor *was* a big teapot that night. All the king's tea was used, but nobody drank a cup of it—nobody paid a penny for it.

The king soon heard of that tea party at Boston and he remembered it! He knew that the fifty men with tomahawks were not Indians. He knew that they were just some men of Boston who were dressed like Indians.

He also knew that the people of Boston would not buy any of his tea—tea with his tax on it.

But the king said: "Those people shall be sorry for that tea party!" And he kept up the quarrel with them till a great war broke out.

That war is known in our history as the Revolutionary War. It made our people free from the king's laws and the king's taxes.

# THE TEA PARTY
# AT EDENTON

You remember about the Boston Tea Party, do you not? That was in December, 1773.

A few months later a famous tea party was held at Edenton, in the Old North State—North Carolina. Edenton is at the head of Albemarle Sound; ships may easily reach the place; and in the days of long ago it was an important tea market.

In those days nearly everybody drank tea. Frequently ladies and gentlemen would meet together and spend an evening talking and drinking tea. Such a party was called a tea party.

But the Boston Tea Party and the Edenton Tea Party were different. At Boston it was a men's party— the ladies did not participate; at Edenton it was a ladies' party, but they did not use any tea!

Don't you think, then, that both those parties were queer? At Boston there was a tea party without ladies; at Edenton there was a tea party without tea!

I have told you about the party at Boston; so I must tell you about the party at Edenton.

The ladies of Edenton, like the men of Boston, were more or less angry. They did not believe that the king's government had a right to tax their tea. In fact, they went so far as to say that the king ought not to tax anything they used unless he let them take part in making the laws.

So the ladies of Edenton had a meeting—a party. Fifty-one of them met at the house of Mrs. Elizabeth King. They elected a chairman and had one speech after another.

One speaker said that she did not think the ladies of Edenton ought to use tea at all while the king was taxing it.

"I, for one," she exclaimed, "will never use it again unless the tax is removed."

Another said that her tea cups should be empty of tea unless the tax were soon taken off. A third declared that she would rather drink tea made of raspberry leaves than of tea that had the British tax on it.

All who spoke seemed to agree that if they should drink tea and pay the hated tax they would be giving up their liberties.

"Therefore," they declared, "we will not drink tea— we will not buy anything from England until the tax is taken off."

Somebody wrote those brave words down, and all the ladies put their fair hands to them. That is to say, each lady signed her name to the paper.

It must have been hard on the people of Edenton to do without tea, but they, like the people of Boston and many other places, did do without it. They drank no more tea, they had no more tea parties, till the Revolutionary War was over and they could buy tea again without paying tax to the king.

# THE FIRST FOURTH OF JULY

One day, more than a hundred years ago, five men were appointed to write a letter to the world. One of the five men was old—seventy years old. His name was Benjamin. Two of them were middle-aged. Their names were John and Roger. The other two were young men, and their names were Robert and Thomas.

Most of the letter was written by one of the young men—by the one named Thomas. He was tall and had sandy hair. His eyes were gray and often sparkled like two stars. He was strong and liked to ride horseback.

Thomas dipped his quill pen into the ink and scratched away on the paper till the letter was finished. When the other four men read it they liked it so well that they asked him to make only a few changes.

Soon after the letter was written a big bell began to ring and men began to throw up their hats and shout. The big bell rang and the people shouted because the letter to the world had been written and signed. It was signed by the five men who wrote it, and also by fifty-one other men who had asked them to write it.

That letter to the world is now known in every part of the world. In the United States of America it is printed in most of the books of history that boys and girls study in school. It is called the Declaration of Independence.

The young man Thomas who wrote the Declaration was Thomas Jefferson. He was afterwards President of the United States. The Declaration was signed on the 4th of July, 1776. That is the reason we celebrate the 4th of July every year. The big bell weighs more than a ton and it is known as Liberty Bell. It still rings now and then for liberty. It is kept in the city where the Declaration of Independence was written and signed.

How many of you know the name of that city? You have all heard the 4th of July called Independence Day. Liberty Bell hangs in Independence Hall, in the city of Philadelphia. Liberty Bell became famous on the first 4th of July in American history.

# CROSSING THE DELAWARE

## (For the Christmas Season)

You have often seen a picture of some soldiers in a boat, with a flag; of big chunks of ice floating in the water; and these words under the picture: "Washington Crossing the Delaware."

I am going to tell you the story of that picture.

The Delaware is a big river that flows down into the Delaware Bay between Pennsylvania and New Jersey. Pennsylvania is on the west side, New Jersey is on the east side.

In the year 1776, during the Revolutionary. War, the British army drove General Washington and his little army down from New York, clear across the state of New Jersey, across the Delaware River, into the state of Pennsylvania. If Washington had not gathered up all the boats for many miles up and down the river and taken them over to his side, the British would have crossed the river after him, into Pennsylvania.

As it was, the British thought they were rid of Washington, and they believed that the war would soon be over. One of the British generals began to pack his trunks and get ready to go back to England. He thought the war was just about ended.

But the war was not over, although the American people were much discouraged, and although the American soldiers were ragged, hungry, and cold. Washington decided that a big Christmas gift would do all of his people good, and he proceeded to get them one. That is the reason he crossed the Delaware—he went back into New Jersey to get the Americans a Christmas gift.

It was Christmas night. At Trenton, over in New Jersey, a thousand men were sleeping. They were German soldiers, Hessians, fighting under the British flag. They had eaten their Christmas puddings, they had drunk their Christmas wine; they had laughed and danced and sung; now they were fast asleep. Washington crossed the Delaware to get those thousand men.

But crossing the Delaware was a hard job. The weather was bitter cold. The river was wide and the water was cold as ice. Big cakes of ice were floating in the water. It was hard to keep them from smashing the boats. The wind blew its freezing breath across the valley, and towards midnight snow and sleet began to fall.

In Washington's little army were some sailors and fishermen. They had often been out on the cold waters; they had often battled with winter storms. They rowed the boats that carried Washington and his men across the Delaware.

But they found it no easy task, and it took them ten long hours. The army began crossing about dark. Back and forth across the wide river, dodging the cakes of ice, the strong fishermen rowed the boats; but it was four o'clock in the morning before all the soldiers were across.

The men who got across first had to wait nearly all night for the others to come. They could not make fires for fear the enemy's pickets would see them, so they tried to keep from freezing by walking back and forth upon the frozen ground. As it was, two men died from cold before they got to Trenton, nine miles away.

It was daylight before Washington and his men reached Trenton; but the enemy were still asleep.

Washington's army entered Trenton from two sides. They drove in the British pickets, planted their cannon so as to sweep the streets, and fixed their bayonets. Then a gun boomed out and the enemy began to wake up.

But it was too late. As the Hessians rushed out into the streets, many of them still half asleep, they looked into the mouths of Washington's cannon and ran against the sharp points of the American bayonets. Their commander fell mortally wounded and they had to surrender.

Washington then went back across the Delaware into Pennsylvania. But he took with him a thousand prisoners. They were his Christmas gift to the American cause. It came the day after Christmas, but our people were just as glad to receive it and were encouraged by it just as much as if it had come the day before Christmas.

Whenever you see that picture, "Washington Crossing the Delaware," you will not forget how brave the deed was, and how much Washington and his men suffered that Christmas night to help their country.

# CYNTHIA'S COW

Cynthia Smith was a little girl who lived in South Carolina more than a hundred years ago. When the war of the Revolution began she was just seven years old.

Cynthia had a pet calf. It was red and white, and Cynthia thought it was very pretty. She and the calf were great friends.

When the Declaration of Independence was signed Cynthia was eight, and when some one read the Declaration she listened eagerly. In the Declaration are two words that she liked very much. They are "free" and "equal."

"Free 'n Equal!" cried Cynthia; "I'm going to name my calf "Free 'n Equal!"

And so she did. "Free 'n Equal" learned to know her name and seemed well pleased with it.

Toward the end of the war General Cornwallis, a British general, led his army of Red-coats into South Carolina. They came and camped near Cynthia's home. Cynthia by that time was eleven or twelve years old—a good-sized girl; and how about "Free 'n Equal"?

# Cynthia's Cow

"Free 'n Equal" was no longer a calf—she was a fine cow. She supplied Cynthia and her mother with good milk; but she was still a pet. She and Cynthia were still close friends.

One day when Cynthia came home from an errand "Free 'n Equal" was gone. Where do you think she was?

The Red-coats had come and had driven her away. They had taken her to their camp, for they, too, liked good milk.

Cynthia cried bitterly. She was almost heartbroken. She felt that she could not give up her cow, yet she did not know how to get her back.

At last she said: "Mother, I am going to see General Cornwallis and ask him to let me bring 'Free 'n Equal' home."

Her mother said, "Child, it is no use. He won't let you have her." But finally she gave her consent, and off Cynthia trudged. She had to walk three miles over a hot and dusty road to reach the British camp.

Why didn't Cynthia's father or one of her brothers go? Can't you guess?

Her father and her five brothers were away from home. They were off with the American army, trying to get a chance to drive the Red-coats out of the country. Cynthia and her mother were at home alone.

Poor Cynthia's heart beat fast and her courage almost failed her, but she trudged on. In the British camp were so many soldiers with their guns and bayonets and swords that Cynthia was frightened worse than ever. "But," she thought, "it won't do to give up now."

"Where is General Cornwallis?" she inquired.

Then she was led before the great general.

"Little girl," said he, "what do you want?"

Cynthia tried hard not to let her voice tremble, but it did tremble just a little as she replied:

"General, your soldiers have stolen my cow, and I want you to give her back to me."

Then she told him how much she and her mother needed "Free 'n Equal."

The general listened kindly to what Cynthia said. He smiled a little when she told him that her cow's name was "Free 'n Equal."

"You are a sturdy little rebel," he declared, "and you shall have your cow."

So Cynthia went back home happy.

General Cornwallis not only sent back Cynthia's cow—he also gave her a pair of silver knee-buckles, such as gentlemen then wore, as a present. Cynthia kept those buckles all her life. Whenever she looked at them she remembered how the British general had called her a "sturdy little rebel" and a "brave little woman."

# OPENING THE
# GOLDEN GATE

One summer day a ship turned its head slowly toward the east. It was the ship *Saint Charles*. Its captain was a Spaniard, Don John.

As his ship turned toward the east—toward the land—Don John saw a mountain on the right. He also saw a mountain on the left. But between the two mountains was a wide path of beautiful blue water. His ship sailed slowly in on the wide path of blue water, between the two mountains.

After he had sailed in five or six miles Don John saw the blue water widen out before him into a splendid, big harbor.

Don John had found the Golden Gate! He had sailed in through the Golden Gate into the great harbor of San Francisco.

That was more than a hundred years ago, and no city was there then; but we may say that Don John opened the Golden Gate, for ships have been sailing in ever since.

After a while the people of the United States hoisted the Stars and Stripes at the Golden Gate. Then, just a year or two later, they found real gold up in the hills near by and along the rivers that flow down and meet the ocean at the Golden Gate. Then thousands of people rushed toward the Golden Gate from all over the world, and San Francisco grew as if a fairy had touched it with a magic wand. Soon it was a city. The hills and the sea had been lying there quiet for ages and ages; now every bird that passed and every breeze that stirred the blue waters seemed to say, "Awake! awake!"

Eggs were a dollar apiece. A bed cost five dollars a night. A hired man was paid twenty dollars a day. Nobody could afford to sleep any longer.

In 1915 thousands of people from all over the world flocked to the Golden Gate again. This time they went to attend a great fair—the Panama-Pacific Exposition. Another gate for ships had been opened at Panama, and all the world rejoiced. The nations met together at San Francisco to shake hands and to see the wonders.

Nature made the Golden Gate. The Golden Gate, ever since the day Don John opened it, has been making history.

# THE STAR-SPANGLED BANNER

One morning a teacher and his class entered a large building in Washington City, just at nine o'clock. They had gone to the capital of our nation to study history.

They had visited Mt. Vernon, the old home of Washington, and Arlington, the old home of Robert E. Lee. They had gone through the great capitol building and the beautiful Library of Congress. They had heard the United States Marine Band give a concert on the White House lawn. Now they were going into the National Museum. This was the large building they entered at nine o'clock that morning—as soon as the doors opened.

They found the Museum the most interesting place of all, perhaps. They saw old letters that had been written by famous men; old pistols and swords that had belonged to famous soldiers; old jackets and coats that had been worn in times past; old pieces of machinery that had been wonders in their day. For example, they saw a little old railway engine that was used on one of the first railroads in this country.

All at once one of the girls called the teacher, and soon the whole party was gathered close around a large glass case. In the case was a big old flag. The colors were not bright any more, but it was still easy to see what was red, what was white, and what was blue.

"Those stripes are a foot wide," said Walter.

"Yes," replied Janet, "and the stars are as big as my hat."

"I wonder how large the whole flag is," remarked Virginia.

"Here is a card that tells us," answered Orena; "it is twenty-seven feet wide and thirty-two feet long."

"It surely is a whopper," exclaimed John; "it's almost big enough to cover the side of a barn."

"In the year 1814," said the teacher, "it was big enough to cover Baltimore."

The boys and girls looked puzzled, so the teacher went on:

"You remember that a few days ago in school we learned to sing our national anthem, 'The Star-Spangled Banner.' Last evening the band played it and all the people stood up.

"This song, you know, was written by Francis Scott Key. We passed his house in Georgetown yesterday.

"It was during the War of 1812. The British ships were firing on Baltimore, and Key was a prisoner on one of the ships. Before the British ships could get to Baltimore they had to pass Fort McHenry. But that was not an easy thing to do, for in the fort were a lot of big cannons and they blazed away at the British ships with might and main.

"The sun went down, but the fight went on. Then it began to grow dusk. But the fight went on. At the last gleaming of twilight Mr. Key looked toward Fort McHenry to see whether the American flag was still flying. It was still there. Clouds of battle smoke were in the way, but now and then he could see the broad stripes and the bright stars streaming over the walls of the fort.

"It grew dark, but the fight went on. Mr. Key could not see the fort any longer, but whenever a rocket would shoot up and make a red glare in the sky, or a bomb would burst somewhere in the air, he knew that Fort McHenry was still holding out—that the flag of the fort was still flying.

"But late in the night the noise stopped. Why, Mr. Key did not know. He was afraid that the fort had surrendered—that the flag had been hauled down. He did not sleep much, you may be sure; he was too anxious to know which side had won the battle.

"Before daylight he was up, looking toward the land. Presently it grew lighter, and he could see a little. He could see a big blur on the shore. That, he knew, was the fort. After a while he could see the flagstaff, and he could see that there was a flag on it, but he could not tell yet what flag it was. He thought at first that it might be the British flag—that would have meant that the fort had surrendered—that the British had captured Baltimore.

"All at once the breeze blew the flag out and the sun shone on it. It was not the British flag—it was the 'Star-Spangled Banner'! It was still there! Fort McHenry had won; the city was safe.

"Mr. Key was worked up to such a pitch of joy that he took an old piece of paper that he happened to have in his pocket and wrote on it, right there and then, the words of our grand national song, 'The Star-Spangled Banner.'

"That was a hundred years ago, but this old flag here in the case before us is the flag that Mr. Key saw flying over Fort McHenry; and the song he wrote our people have been singing ever since."

"Let's sing it now," said one of the boys.

The teacher agreed. The whole party stood close together before the faded old flag and sang:

O say! can you see by the dawn's early light
    What so proudly we hailed at the twilight's last gleaming?
Whose broad stripes and bright stars, through the clouds of
    the fight,
O'er the ramparts we watched were so gallantly streaming?
    And the rocket's red glare—the bombs bursting in air
    Gave proof through the night that our flag was still there?
O say, does that star-spangled banner yet wave
O'er the land of the free and the home of the brave?

It was an odd thing to do in the National Museum—to sing that song there, without asking anybody's leave; but nobody offered any objection. To have stopped that song would have been too much like tearing down the flag.

# THE BOY AND THE FLAG

One day a boy saw the flag. It was waving over the schoolhouse. The boy stopped and began to talk to himself. He was thinking of his father and of the flag. His father was in France, wearing Uncle Sam's uniform, following the flag.

Before he had gone to France he had often talked to the boy about the flag; and so as the boy stood and watched the flag and talked to himself he was thinking of what his father had often said to him. This is what the boy said to himself as he watched the flag:

"I believe that our flag has a voice and that it is calling to me. The red speaks for courage, the white speaks for cleanness, the blue speaks for truth. They all speak for good citizenship.

"I believe that the good citizen is square in his dealings, honest in his work, and fair in his play. He pays his taxes without grumbling and casts his vote without cheating. He tries to make the world beautiful instead of ugly, and the people happy rather than unhappy. He looks upon our flag without fear, he rests beneath it without shame; and, for freedom's sake, he dies under it without regret.

"But I believe that living for my country in time of peace is just as much my duty as dying for her in time of war.

"I believe that my country should deal fairly and squarely with other countries; that it has the right to a square deal from them; and that the people of all lands should be friends.

"To know what is true, to do what is just, and to make what is beautiful—this, I believe, is to be a good citizen.

"This, I believe, is the message of our flag — its message to me."

# A CABIN IN KENTUCKY

## (For February 12— Lincoln's Birthday)

Not long ago a great president of the United States went to the state of Kentucky to see a little log cabin. It was because another great president of the United States had been born in that cabin.

The cabin stands in Larue County, Kentucky. A fine house has been built over it to keep it safe and sound, and the Stars and Stripes wave above it every day. In that cabin Abraham Lincoln was born more than a hundred years ago.

To keep this cabin safe, as I said, a large house has been built over it. The whole farm around it has been turned into a park; and, in order that people may visit the place whenever they wish, a good road has been constructed to it.

In the year 1916 the cabin, the fine house over it, and the park around it were given to the United States government, to be kept for all our people. President Woodrow Wilson went to Kentucky to receive this splendid gift.

In that little log cabin Abraham Lincoln was born in the year 1809. At that time the country was full of Indians. His grandfather had been killed by Indians not so many years before.

*"A Cabin in Kentucky"*

The Lincolns were poor, and Abraham as a boy had a hard time. He did not mind working hard, but he did mind being out of school and not having books to read. He had only a few books, and about the only time he had to read them was at night. Then he did not have a good light. Often he would have to sit on the floor, in front of the open fireplace of the cabin, and read the best he could by the flickering blaze. It is a wonder that the smoke and the bad light did not put out his eyes.

But Lincoln kept on studying and working. On one occasion he worked hard in a man's cornfield for three days to pay for a book.

When Lincoln was grown up he became a lawyer. Then he was elected to Congress, and finally he became president of the United States. He made such a strong, wise president that all the nation now honors him. That is the reason why our people now are taking such pains to preserve the little cabin in which he was born; and that is the reason why thousands of persons will visit the Lincoln farm in Kentucky every year, just as they visit Mt. Vernon, the home of Washington.

Near the Lincoln cabin is a spring. The water comes out between ledges of limestone rocks. A good shade is cast over the spring by several fine trees that stand near by. When Lincoln was a boy he often drank at that spring, and I suppose that he often helped his mother carry water from it to the house, which stood not far away.

# THE RIVER THAT RUNS THROUGH A MOUNTAIN

I suppose that all of you have seen a river. I wonder how many of you have seen a mountain? Hands up!

Ralph, who has seen a mountain, may tell us what mountain he has seen, and what a mountain is.

Do you not think it would be strange to see a river that runs through a mountain? Usually creeks and rivers run around hills and mountains, but I am going to tell you about a river that flows right through a mountain.

This river is in the state of Colorado. Long ago it ran down a deep, dark hollow between two high mountains. A hollow or gorge like this is often called a cañon. This gorge in Colorado is so deep and dark that it is called Black Cañon. It is so steep and rocky, and the river runs so swiftly, that the Indians used to be afraid of it. They said that nobody could go through Black Cañon alive.

And it was a long time before anybody did go through Black Cañon. But at last two brave young men went through.

How do you suppose they did it? Other men had tried to go through in boats, but the water was so swift and the rocks were so close that the boats were soon smashed. So these two young men did not go in boats. They climbed along on the rocks wherever they could do so, and whenever they came to a place where they could not hold on any longer they dropped into the cold, swift water and swam down the river till they could find a bank that was not so steep. Climbing and swimming, swimming and climbing, they went on day after day for miles and miles, till at last they got through.

Just across the mountain, not far from Black Cañon on the left-hand side of the river, was a broad, level valley. It was a large country and land was cheap, but nobody bought the land—nobody lived there. The valley had no water—it was a desert.

In Black Cañon was plenty of water and some to spare, but how could anybody get water into the desert from Black Cañon? There was a high mountain between them.

Finally some other brave men went down into Black Cañon with picks and shovels and rock drills and sledges, and they cut a big hole right through the mountain—right through the rocks. In the cañon they started digging even with the water; on the side of the desert they came out lower down, so the water would run through.

Then there was plenty of water in the desert. Now wheat and corn and grass and trees and flowers grow there. Now many people live there and they raise thousands of horses, cattle, hogs, and sheep. Now the whole valley, that was a desert so long, is full of towns, villages, and farms, with orchards of peaches and apples. It is a beautiful valley. It does not get all of the water that flows down Black Cañon, but it gets enough; for in Black Cañon is plenty of water and some to spare. If you were to go into this valley to-day, you would not dream that it ever had been a desert. It is a beautiful valley now because the river runs through the mountain.

Now, before I end this story, I must tell you the name of this river. It is the Gunnison River; and the big hole that lets the water through the mountain is called Gunnison Tunnel.

The river and the tunnel are both named after Captain John Gunnison. He was another brave young man who helped to make the country a good land in which to live. He was first a school teacher; then he became a soldier and a surveyor. Many years ago he was sent into Colorado to mark out a good path for a railroad. Many Indians were then in the country, and one morning early, while he and his men were eating breakfast, the war-whoop was heard. As the young captain stepped to the door of the tent to tell the Indians that he was their friend they fired their rifles and shot their arrows. Fifteen arrows struck him and he fell dead; but he will never be forgotten. In western Colorado his name is spoken every day, in Gunnison County, in Gunnison City, and all along the Gunnison River; and as long as Gunnison River runs through Gunnison Tunnel Captain Gunnison will be remembered.

# THE CROSS ON THE MOUNTAIN

## (For May 18— Peace Day)

For a long time two countries had a quarrel. Two farmers sometimes quarrel over a line fence. These two countries had the same kind of trouble—they were quarreling over their boundary line—the line between their lands. One said, "The line is here"; the other said, "No, it is there."

For many years they quarreled. At the same time they were arming their soldiers and building battleships. It looked as if the quarrel would lead to war.

But at last they said, "How much better it is to be friends! Let us stop our quarreling and let us ask some good men to come and help us find out just where the boundary line ought to be."

So they stopped quarreling and got some good men, who were friends to both parties, to come and fix the line. These men studied the case, looked at both sides, and then fixed the line where they thought it ought to be.

Then both the countries were satisfied. They did not talk any more about war. They did not arm any more soldiers or build any more battleships. They said:

"Now we can have peace—now we can be friends."

Then they said: "Let us erect a monument to show that our quarrel is ended; to show that we are good friends and good neighbors."

So they made a great cross of bronze. Then they met together on the top of a high mountain and set up the cross. On that high mountain, where they once had quarreled, they met as friends, and there they set up the great bronze cross—a sign of peace and good will.

That great bronze cross is standing on that mountain still. I wish I could show you a picture of it. I wish that you all could see it.

And there is more of the monument than I have told you of. The main part of the monument is a figure of Christ, and he holds the cross in his hand.

Now, this is my story of the cross on the mountain; and here is a picture.

Do you not think that those people were wise to settle their trouble as friends, rather than to go to war about it as enemies?

We are hoping that some day all nations will be wise enough to follow their example. We are hoping for a great day of peace for all the world.

*The Cross on the Mountain*
*(The Christ of the Andes)*

In a beautiful city across the sea is a splendid building called the Temple of Peace. There good men and women from many lands have met, from time to time, working and praying for peace. In our schools every year, when the 18th of May comes round, we have a day called Peace Day. The boys and girls in our schools are learning that peace is better than war.

Every Christmas Day is a peace day, too, for then the people all remember a sweet song of peace that the angels sang:

> Glory to God in the highest,
> Peace on earth, good will to men!

We all are hoping for a glad, good day, soon to come, when the whole world can join the angels' song. That will be Peace Day indeed. Then the people of every land can meet as friends. Then, in truth, upon the highest mountain a cross may be erected, and the Prince of Peace will hold it up.

# NOTES

THE FIRST CHRISTMAS SONG—There are many simple, beautiful Christmas songs that may be sung with the children at this season in connection with this story and others of similar character.

THE GIRL WHO HEARD VOICES—Joan of Arc is one of the most wonderful figures in history. She came from the village of Domremy, in the northeast of France, not far from historic Verdun. She led the French at Orléans in April, 1429; she had the young king crowned in the old cathedral at Rheims in the following July; in May, 1430, she fell into the hands of the enemy; in May, 1431, she was burned at the stake in Rouen. She was only nineteen when she died.

THANKSGIVING DAY—This story will be appropriate at any time within the Thanksgiving season. You should have at hand as many as possible of the particular things mentioned in the story: A calendar, with large figures on it; several ears of corn,—white, yellow, and red; apples; walnuts; shellbarks (and other hickory nuts); acorns; and a pumpkin or two. All these things may be collected during the month of November. They should be kept at hand until all the children are familiar with them. They will be useful in connection with all the Thanksgiving studies of the season.

WASHINGTON'S BIRTHDAY—The first home, where Washington was born, was on Bridge's Creek Plantation in Westmoreland County, Virginia. The second was on or near Hunting Creek in Fairfax County. This was known as the Washington Plantation; later it was named Mt. Vernon. The third was in Stafford County, opposite or nearly opposite Fredericksburg.

This story follows an account supposed to be reliable, though some accounts contain no reference to the sojourn at Hunting Creek.

A BIG BELL—See whether any of the children will ask the name of the city in which Liberty Bell is kept. It is usually kept in Philadelphia, in Independence Hall.

BETSY ROSS'S NEEDLE—The Old Flag House, in which Betsy Ross lived, stands at 239 Arch Street, Philadelphia. If possible, have some pictures and a flag when you tell this story. Try to have two flags—one like those Mrs. Ross made, another of the present design.

PLANTING A TREE—General Grant made his tour around the world from 1877 to 1880. The tree referred to in this story was planted in Suwa Park, in the city of Nagasaki.

YELLOW KING CORN—This story will be appropriate for either spring or fall. In the autumn you will be able to get more attractive materials to illustrate it. For example, you may have an armful of corn stalks, with tassels and ripe ears, set up in one corner of the room. On the table you may have half a dozen nice ears of yellow corn. In the drawer of your desk you may have two or three white ears and a red ear. Bring these out at the proper moment.

WHITE KING COTTON—In a cotton country this story will need but little illustration. Out of a cotton country cotton plants may sometimes be available. The next best things are pictures. These may be obtained easily anywhere.

STRONG KING IRON—If you have access to a museum and can show the children a stone ax alongside a modern steel ax, the effect will be helpful. Several visits to places where iron is used, manufactured, or mined would be appropriate in this connection. A trip to a hardware store or to a machine shop will be very interesting.

CHUCKY JACK AND HIS HORN—John Sevier was born in Virginia in 1744 or 1745. He died in Alabama in 1815, while there on a mission from President Madison to the Creek Indians. In 1889 his remains were brought back to Tennessee and interred on the court square in Knoxville. He was one of the leading pioneers of Tennessee.

DAVY CROCKETT AND THE BEARS—David Crockett was born in Tennessee in 1786. He fought in the Creek War, and after serving in the state legislature was elected to Congress. In 1835 he went to Texas. There, in March of the next year, he fell in the fight at the Alamo. Karns's "Tennessee History Stories" will be found interesting in respect to Crockett, Sevier, and other famous pioneers.

CHARLES THE GREAT—Charles the Great (Charlemagne) lived from 742 to 814 A.D. His dominions included, in a general way, what are now France and Germany, with other parts of Europe. He was crowned Emperor on Christmas Day, 800, by the Pope (bishop of Rome). Other persons at his court assumed names famous in history and literature.

ALFRED THE GREAT—Alfred the Great lived just a hundred years after Charles the Great and was much like him in many ways.

HOW A KING GOT OUT OF PRISON—Richard I (Lion-Heart) was king of England from 1189 to 1199. In 1190 he started to the Holy Land on a crusade. In the autumn of 1192, while on his return, he was seized and imprisoned by Leopold, Duke of Austria. He finally got back to England in March, 1194.

FINDING A NEW WORLD—Since this story is intended for small children, it has been simplified in many respects. Be sure that the class understands that the Turks are people—not domestic fowls. If anybody wants to know the name of the city captured by the Turks (Constantinople, in 1453), tell it; but do not make the long name a required burden here.

In connection with this story you may develop others from other connected incidents or phases; for example, you may tell one day of the hardships Columbus endured before Queen Isabella helped him. On another day you may go into the details of the voyage; on another you may give an account of the landing of Columbus and the planting of the cross; and on still another you may portray the grand reception that was given Columbus on his return to Spain.

Practically all the stories in this book may be used as the starting places for other related stories.

THE MAYFLOWER AND THE PILGRIMS—It will not be difficult to get attractive pictures of Plymouth, Plymouth Rock, the canopy over the Rock, and other objects of interest in connection with the landing of the Pilgrims.

RIDING A COLT—See whether any of the children

will inquire about Washington's father. His father was dead—he had died when George was about eleven years old. At the time of this incident the family was living near Fredericksburg, Virginia.

PLANTING THIRTEEN TREES—The author is indebted to Mr. Isaac Markens and Dr. Allan McLane Hamilton for some of the foregoing facts relating to the Grange and the Thirteen Trees. Both of these gentlemen live in New York City, and the latter is a grandson of Alexander Hamilton.

A HOUSE ON A MOUNTAIN—The educated people at Charlottesville pronounce Monticello "Montichello."

ROBERT LEE AND HIS MOTHER—Gilman's life of Robert E. Lee is interesting.

A BOY'S BOAT-RIDE—Lincoln started on this trip from a point on the Ohio River near Rockport, Indiana, not far above Evansville. Sketch an outline map on the board to show the general plan of the route and the location of New Orleans. The place where the fight with the robbers occurred was near Baton Rouge. Pictures of flatboats and steamboats will be helpful in connection with this story.

A SWEET SONG—If possible sing "Home, Sweet Home" for the children; then have them join in. They will not at this stage of their development appreciate all of the words, but they will learn the melody and will get some of the spirit of the song. John Howard Payne was born in New York in 1791; he died in Africa in 1852. In 1882, W. W. Corcoran had his remains brought to America and buried in Oak Hill Cemetery, Washington, D.C. The simple and sufficient inscription on his monument is: "John Howard Payne, Author of 'Home, Sweet Home.' The dates, etc., are only incidental.

SAINT VALENTINE—You may be able to make a collection of attractive valentines a few days before the 14th, and tell this story in time for the children to put it to the test. If you can get one or two of the old-fashioned, handmade valentines they will prove very interesting in this connection.

BALBOA'S DISCOVERY—Balboa's discovery was made in 1513. The Panama-Pacific Exposition was held in 1915. The town of Balboa Heights is at the southern end of the Canal Zone, at the point where the Canal enters the Pacific.

THE MAN WHO WAS THIRSTY—John Ponce is, of course, Juan Ponce de Leon.

JAMESTOWN DAY—In Clifton Johnson's "Highways and Byways of the South" will be found a very delightful account of a visit to Jamestown a few years ago.

A CITY ON A ROCK—It is said that Quebec was the Indian name for "the narrows" in the river, and that they pronounced it *Kebec*. For some time an Indian village by the name of Stadacona had stood at the place.

WHEN NEW YORK CITY HAD A WALL—As an aid in telling this story, draw on the blackboard a simple outline map, like the one in the story. If you have a red piece of chalk, use that to indicate the line of the wall.

HOW THANKSGIVING GREW—Washington was inaugurated first in New York City, April 30, 1789. The national capital was there till the latter part of the next year. In December, 1790, it was set up at Philadelphia, where it remained for ten years. In 1800 it was established at Washington.

A FAMOUS TREE—Pictures of the Charter Oak, of Washington's Elm, and of other famous trees will be interesting in connection with this story and in connection with Arbor Day.

THE TEA PARTY AT EDENTON—The Boston Tea Party took place on the night of December 16, 1773; the Edenton Tea Party was held on October 25, 1774. Allen's "North Carolina History Stories" will be found to contain many stirring accounts of incidents in the Old North State.

THE FIRST FOURTH OF JULY—The five members of the committee that drafted the Declaration of Independence were Thomas Jefferson, Benjamin Franklin, John Adams, Roger Sherman, and Robert Livingston. The house in which Jefferson is said to have written the document is still to be seen in Philadelphia, near Independence Hall, and not far from Carpenters Hall and the Betsy Ross house.

CYNTHIA'S COW—Before telling this story it will be well to have a brief preliminary study with the children in the effort to give them some notion of each of the following: The Revolution; the Declaration of Independence; Red-coats.

Make it all very simple. Say, for example: The Revolution was a war to make this country free. Before the Revolution we were under the flag of England; after the Revolution we had a flag of our own. The Declaration of Independence is a long letter that our people wrote soon after the Revolution started. In this letter they said that they wanted to be free and they also stated the reasons why they wanted to be free. The Red-coats were the British soldiers— the soldiers of England. They wore red coats.

THE STAR-SPANGLED BANNER—If you can take the boys and girls once in a while on a short trip to Washington or to some other historic place it will help them more in history and geography than a whole month spent in mere book work. The lines in the story, the first stanza of "The Star-Spangled Banner," are not in the usual form, but they are almost exactly as Mr. Key first wrote them.

A CABIN IN KENTUCKY—The gift of the Lincoln farm to the nation was formally accepted by President Wilson on September 4, 1916. In "Highways and Byways of the South" Mr. Clifton Johnson has a very interesting chapter on the birthplace of Lincoln. It is illustrated with several attractive pictures.

THE RIVER THAT RUNS THROUGH A MOUNTAIN— In this story the correlation of geography and history is prominent.

THE CROSS ON THE MOUNTAIN—The cross on the mountain is on one of the high Andes ranges, on the boundary line between Chile and Argentina. The monument was unveiled March 13, 1904. The whole figure is called the Christ of the Andes. On the monument is this inscription:

"Sooner shall these mountains crumble unto dust, than Argentines and Chilians break the peace which at the feet of Christ the Redeemer they have sworn to maintain."

The Temple of Peace is at the Hague in the Netherlands. The first great peace conference met at the Hague on May 18, 1899. Many organizations are doing much to promote the right kind of peace through the schools.

We say the "right kind of peace." No peace can be real or lasting that is not founded on truth and justice. It must square with right and the rights of man.